# THE MANAGEMENT OF RACIAL INTEGRATION IN BUSINESS

*The following individuals conducted the study
on which this report is based, and are solely responsible
for the contents of the report and for the opinions
and conclusions expressed herein:*

RICHARD D. ALEXANDER

DAVID K. BRAUN

TIMOTHY T. DAY

DORSEY C. DUNN

L. MICHAEL FOLEY

WALTER S. FOSTER

CARTAN B. KRAFT

JERRY D. LAMBO

ROBERT H. MASSON

RICHARD J. RYAN

BERTHOLD H. WALDORF

# THE MANAGEMENT OF RACIAL INTEGRATION IN BUSINESS

*Prepared under the supervision of*

**Georges F. Doriot,** *Professor of Industrial Management*
*Harvard Graduate School of Business Administration*

M c G R A W - H I L L   B O O K   C O M P A N Y

*New York*   *San Francisco*   *Toronto*   *London*

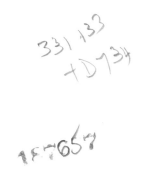

THE MANAGEMENT OF RACIAL INTEGRATION IN BUSINESS

# PREFACE

As a recognized top-priority issue for American business, the
problem of integrating the Negro worker at all levels in U.S. industry
is relatively new--so new, indeed, that few written studies on the subject are available. Much of the existing literature, consisting to a
great extent of unpublished theses and magazine articles, is either in-
accessible or of limited practical usefulness to the businessman. In
undertaking our study of this crucial current problem, therefore, we
turned to field interviews as our main source of information, gathering
our data primarily through discussions in depth with numerous local
and national Negro leaders, government officials, and executives of
approximately sixty-five business organizations. These interviews
ranged from one to six hours in duration, averaging about two and one-
half hours each.

Contacts with the government and with Negro leaders were made
directly; the business organizations, however, were initially approached
through a letter to the presidents describing the purpose of the study
and asking the cooperation of the management individuals best qualified
to discuss the companies' activities and problems with respect to
racial integration. This approach, we believe, largely accounts for the
candid and productive relationships that we were able to develop with
staff and operating management people.

One of our primary criteria in selecting companies for inclusion in this study was their breadth of first-hand experience in dealing with problems of integration. Though we attempted to balance our interviews between large and small firms, our criteria of selection led us to establish contact with a heavy proportion of medium- and large-sized organizations. Because of the qualitative nature of this study, however, our conclusions should be no less applicable to smaller businesses.

Geographically, our survey included formal interviews, arranged for as described above, in the metropolitan areas of Boston, New York City, Washington, D. C., Philadelphia, Pittsburgh, Cleveland, and Detroit. Although our field work did not extend to the South and West, many national companies reported their experiences in implementing company-wide integration policies in Southern and Western plants or offices. Most of these experiences suggest that the problems in the South, through more formidable in magnitude, are nevertheless susceptible to the same techniques of solution as those in the North.

Our study has been an enlightening one, and its implications may well extend beyond U. S. industry's immediate concern with the Negro worker. Though we have specifically dealt with Negroes and whites in America, the substitution of other protagonists may not necessarily reduce the relevance of the problems or the applicability of the techniques described. In fact, the relationships in many countries abroad between people of different races, religions, or national origins have numerous points in common with those between whites and Negroes in the United States. It is our hope that, wherever similar problems exist, our study may prove useful to those who seek constructive solutions.

A note about the authors of this report may be in order. Of our eleven members, all but two have either had full-time business experience or have served three or more years as commissioned officers in the United States Armed Forces. In addition, our work with Professor Georges F. Doriot of the Harvard Business School has enabled us as a group to work with and study the operating problems of two Boston manufacturing firms during the course of an academic year. We hope that this grounding in practical operating problems, both before and during our Business School experience, has qualified us as objective, as well as informed, observers of such problems as those involved in integrating the Negro into all functional areas and levels of business.

The authors are, inevitably, greatly in the debt of many individuals who willingly took time from their busy schedules to share with us the experiences and lessons of their organizations. Our appreciation, however, must be expressed in general terms, since we felt it necessary to conduct our interviews in confidence in order to ensure a candid and extensive elaboration of sensitive issues.

We are deeply indebted to Professor Doriot, for whom this graduate study was originally undertaken, and who impressed upon us the importance of selecting a topic of genuine significance to the businessman of today and tomorrow. We are especially indebted to him for the additional challenge and satisfaction of working on such a topic under his guidance. However, it should be pointed out here that this report expresses only the opinions and conclusions of the authors and not necessarily those of the Harvard Business School or of Professor Doriot.

We owe appreciation, also, to James Henderson, Course Assistant, whose helpful counsel has frequently clarified our direction and facilitated our progress. To Miss Charlotte White, who assisted in the final rewriting, and to our typist, Mrs. Constance Rundlett, go our special thanks. And last, but far from least, we are grateful to our wives for their typing and editing assistance and their encouragement throughout the duration of our study.

*The Authors*

# CONTENTS

# INTRODUCTION

A list of the printed material available in the latter part of 1963 on the subject of broadening the Negro's integration into business would have included a wide range of media and approaches. Articles on the subject appeared frequently in daily newspapers and national magazines, although most of the writing about integration was being directed at its social, political and moral implications. A few unpublished works occupied space on library shelves, but those over four years old were already suffering from obsolescence. Articles available in reprint form from various management periodicals usually proved to be concerned substantially either with the social aspects of the problem or with only a single area, such as recruiting.

It is the authors' conviction that a relatively small sample of American businesses had dealt firsthand with the forces of integration, and that even these few pioneering companies had not yet experienced its full force. As the interaction between these companies and the Negro community continued to develop, more and more areas of the companies' business would be affected, and the experience gap between these firms and other members of the American business community would be increased. Unless the lessons of their frequently painful development were collected and preserved, the companies which would later elect—or be forced—to undertake a similar program would be vulnerable to the same costly errors already encountered and overcome by their predecessors.

The need for a study that would transcend the limitation of existing published materials was gratifyingly confirmed by the cooperation the authors have received—cooperation that exceeded all initial expectations. The willingness of nearly all interviewees to respond to questions in meaningful, specific terms—terms which, in numerous instances were not at all flattering to the organization of the individual involved—could not have been anticipated even by the most optimistic member of the interviewing team. So, while the reader may not agree with all the conclusions or recommendations developed in this report, it is hoped that he will still consider the factual framework to be worthwhile reading.

The study begins with a consideration of the fundamental question of whether to undertake an active integration program. Chapters 2 through 6 discuss five critical areas of the implementation process. It is hoped that the variety of illustrations and ideas presented in these five chapters will enable a company which has decided to embark on a more active integration program to avoid some of the major pitfalls experienced by firms contributing to this study. Ideas should be adopted or disregarded as appears most appropriate in the case of each individual company.

Chapter 7 presents two case illustrations. The episode of the Second National Bank illustrates an ineffective handling of a situation which could have just as easily resulted in a mutually agreeable solution. The Maxwell case exemplifies a more successful solution, achieved at minimum expense in terms of minimization of bad relations, frayed tempers, and wasted time and money.

Finally, Chapter 8 discusses some present trends and the authors' interpretation of their possible meaning and significance.

# — 1

# BUSINESS AND THE PRESSURES
# FOR INTEGRATION

An analysis of the varying efforts of American business to meet the growing challenge of racial integration elicits the disturbing impression that decisions governing such efforts are often based on shallow and even biased research. In a significant number of the cases studied, there appeared to be little effective communication between management and Negroes, either within the business itself or within the community at large. In fact, few representatives of management showed any clear understanding of what it means or how it feels to be a Negro in America, or of what the Negro is currently seeking.

The lack of communication between Negro and white is certainly not peculiar to American business. It is a cleavage deeply and historically rooted in our society as a whole. But as pressures are increasingly brought to bear on closing this gap, the tacit if not official attitude of business seems to be that it is not its role to take a firm and thoughtfully considered stand. Leaving the issue largely to church, school, private, and government programs, a major portion of the business community treats integration as essentially a moral question, not within the scope of business policy. It has indeed signed various

Plans for Progress and in many cases instituted, with sincerity, limited integration programs.* But, in general, business—either as a social or an economic institution—has not fully confronted the problems of integration.

It is the thesis of this study that the failure of business to realistically assess current developments in the area of racial integration is becoming increasingly hazardous. While in the past a policy of subordinating the importance of racial integration to that of other business objectives has seemingly resulted in few negative repercussions, it will not continue to do so. Negro organizations, as well as federal and state governments, are creating pressures which can no longer prudently be ignored. If business seeks to cope adequately with a changing environment, it must take a new and objective look at Negro demands. The reappraisal will involve a fundamental, and in many cases unpleasant, reevaluation of principles, beliefs, and practices. This study attempts to suggest factors which should be considered in the process. The following points seem particularly cogent to an understanding of the increasing need to develop comprehensive integration policies now.

## The Inevitability of Integration

Among those American companies with advanced integration programs, a major reason given for their efforts is that integration seems to them inevitable. They feel that unless they act on their own now, they will be forced to do so at a later date under less favorable conditions. Acutely sensitive to the implications of the growing militancy and power of Negro groups, they have taken decisive steps in the long-range training of Negroes for positions at all levels. Unlike many of their peers and competitors, they seem to grasp the Negroes' need not only for just monetary compensation but for the opportunity to gain the prerogatives and responsibilities of management positions. Since most such positions require years of training, Negro trainees must be sought and assimilated now if the companies wish to be inte-

*For details about the Plans for Progress Program, see Exhibit #1 of the Appendix.

grated in the future. The failure of most executives to accept the inevitability of integration or prepare for assimilating Negroes into management positions is aptly exemplified today by the banking industry, where there are almost no Negro credit analysts or loan officers.

## Adverse Effects of Discrimination on Management and Company Morale

On several occasions, members of management have referred to a recent Harvard Business Review study by Garda W. Bowman concerning the character of capable management.* In this article, Dr. Bowman showed a correlation between poor managers and managers who were prejudiced against minority groups. It is, says Dr. Bowman, the inclination of prejudice to give undue weight to factors which have no actual bearing on job performance. Under prejudiced management, candidates for promotion must satisfy certain requirements of race, nationality, and social standing before the other factors which most executives rate as relevant come into play. Not only does discrimination seriously affect company morale; it costs the company the opportunity to gain or promote many able employees.

Of even greater importance, according to a few executives, prejudice may become structured within the hierarchical order of the company, coloring its approach to a variety of problems and reinforcing, in turn, the existence of prejudice itself. Biased analysis conceivably leads to poor management decisions, thereby weakening management's ability to handle adequately a variety of related problems. It is significant that Dr. Bowman's study also showed that nearly two-thirds of the businessmen interviewed felt that Negroes had less opportunity for advancement in their own company. The study further indicated that a man's degree of upward mobility may be significantly influenced by such other factors as religion, national origin and educational background.

---

*Garda W. Bowman, "What Helps or Harms Promotability?" Harvard Business Review, January-February 1964, pp. 6-8ff.

## Common Interests Between Business and Negroes

Some companies have emphasized the cost of preventing minority groups from obtaining jobs commensurate with their abilities, a cost estimated by the President's Economic Council to equal $17 billion in reduced Gross National Product a year. These companies feel that if business does not better utilize Negro abilities, the public will support increasingly expensive welfare projects to subsidize the Negro standard of living, with business in turn forced to pay increased taxes.

Although an integrative program adopted by an individual company may produce a negligible impact on the level of federal taxes or the state of the national economy, it can prove to be demonstrably significant locally. By expanding the local employment opportunities for minority groups, even a single company can help materially to reduce social unrest, encourage new investment in the area, and promote the prosperity and growth of the community.

## Value of Negro Markets

Most companies agree that hiring Negroes aids them in capitalizing on Negro markets. They feel, for example, that Negro marketing executives may understand better than whites what advertising slogans and media will most effectively appeal to the Negro community. Other companies reason that Negro administrators make their product more acceptable, and that Negro consumers are more likely to listen to Negro salesmen. A company that hires Negro employees, they reason, builds good will in the Negro community.

## Threat of Government Intervention

The majority of the companies interviewed recognized the recent, rapid increase of the influence of both local and federal government in the area of civil rights. In fact, over 28 states and 50 municipalities have passed fair employment practice laws containing varying degrees of enforcement powers. While most of these laws have been loosely implemented, it would take only a change in the degree of enforcement to make them much more effective.

Government contractors emphasized the significance of the President's Committee on Equal Employment Opportunity, established by executive order on March 6, 1961. Formerly headed by then Vice-President Johnson, this Committee's primary function is to enforce the standard government nondiscrimination clause. Under this clause, all contractors agree to take "affirmative" action to insure that a nondiscriminatory policy applies among their employees. Although the Committee has publicly banned only two companies from further government contracts pending remedial action, many contractors attest that the mere possibility of loss of government business has in most cases been a strong inducement to eliminate discriminatory practices. The President's Committee on Equal Employment Opportunity has also encouraged voluntary compliance beyond the minimum levels acceptable by the Committee through its "Plans for Progress" program. This voluntary program, open to all companies, requires its members to agree to various measures for promoting merit employment. These measures include an original "Plan for Progress" with subsequent self-evaluation reports.

Many of the company executives interviewed felt that, in addition to the regulative activities of the President's Committee, federal racial integration legislation similar to the current Civil Rights Bill would be expanded considerably. These executives recognize that the Federal Government has many means of control over most businesses, and they feel that public sentiment will force government intervention if business fails to integrate on its own.

## The Nature of Boycotts

A few companies discern a fundamental shift in Negro agitation from the courts to the streets. They feel that Negroes are convinced their demands are just, and that only legal delays and white intransigence prevent rapid corrections of past inequities. Court decisions frequently take years to formulate and decades to enforce. The efficacy of the Civil Rights Act of 1964 has yet to be determined. Even the executive branch of the Government is, in the opinion of the Negroes, too dependent on white votes to bring about any rapid changes.

Instead, Negroes now feel they must rely on an appeal to the fundamental concepts guaranteed by the Bill of Rights. The same respect for vehement minority opinions which accepts Senate filibusters permits demonstrations and even the technically illegal boycotts, or so-called "selective patronage" campaigns. As long as demonstrations do not alienate whites so strongly that they actively try to suppress the demonstrations, Negroes regard active white support for demonstrations as unnecessary. White acceptance of Negro demonstrations offers companies few real alternatives in their attempts to resist Negro demands. As the president of one boycotted bank put it, "I never knew I had so few friends." All his competitors privately encouraged him to fight the Negro demonstrations, while they publicly supported the need for increased integration and hired additional Negroes for high-visibility positions in their own firms.

In proportion to the increasing vulnerability of business to Negro demands, the Negroes themselves have increased the efficiency of their own organizations. For example, within 18 months after their first demonstration in Boston, Negro leaders in the area greatly increased their ability to deal with local companies. At first they issued a warning to managements before demonstrating. However, experience indicated that this approach was both time-consuming and ineffective. Most businesses denied that they had ever discriminated and the demonstrators found themselves in the difficult position of trying to prove discrimination without access to company records. Furthermore, managements tended to take few, if any, preventive steps in the way of initiating integration on their own, knowing that the preliminary warning would give them an opportunity to consider carefully whether to accede to Negro demands or to prepare to counteract a boycott. Today, however, some of these same organizations feel confident enough of their position to boycott or picket first and then begin negotiations with a more malleable management.

Clearly, the businesses most vulnerable to Negro purchase boycotts are consumer-goods companies, particularly those which sell largely undifferentiated repeat-purchase products such as bread, milk, soft drinks, and gasoline through retail outlets and/or home

8

deliverymen. Boycotts affect sales of these companies quickly and are successful largely because consumers can so easily substitute another brand or shop at another store. Sales of a midwestern bread company fell between 15% and 40% during one boycott. The former estimate was provided by management; the latter by a spokesman for the Negro group which conducted the campaign. Even after the boycott was over, sales remained lower than normal as many customers failed to return to the boycotted product. A sales decline of even 15% would hurt the morale of commissioned salesmen in most companies, and in high fixed cost industries it could significantly reduce profits.

Occasionally, only one of the many products of a large corporation may become vulnerable to selective buying tactics. Many otherwise invulnerable chemical companies are now vulnerable because of their diversification into consumer products. One large manufacturing concern was relatively immune to boycotts until one of its subsidiaries came out with a hair straightener.

Although non-repeat-purchase products such as automobiles or clothes are now difficult to boycott, they may eventually become vulnerable if Negroes succeed in establishing an effective nationwide organization. Even construction supplies could eventually be boycotted through picketing at new sites where the contractor is using particular brands of building materials.

Utilities, transportation companies, and many other service organizations are vulnerable to demonstrations because of their need for close contact with, if not the cooperation of, their consumers. As a customer service, the telephone company provides extra trunk lines to handle peak load long distance calls. A coordinated effort to overload long-distance capacity with fictitious calls would prevent legitimate calls from being completed. Also, airlines, hotels, and other businesses relying on telephone reservations could be seriously inconvenienced by false reservations, preventing legitimate customers from obtaining proper service.

Though not all companies recognize their vulnerability to boycotts, all are probably vulnerable to at least some form of harassment. Again, business telephones can easily be tied up with fictitious calls

9

during the day and the private phones of management people can be deluged with "wrong number" calls during the night. Public buildings, such as observation towers and even office buildings, can be effectively cut off from the public by aggressive picketing.

## *The Question of Morality*

Almost all executives interviewed believed integration to be morally right and felt an obligation to encourage it. Despite this point of general agreement, however, there were notable discrepancies in the extent to which different companies did in fact integrate. Perhaps because of the difficulty of justifying business decisions on moral grounds, those companies that seemed to emphasize the moral aspects of racial integration generally accomplished the least.

Attacking discrimination within business on moral grounds may make it harder to convince others within the business community of the practical need for racial integration. And, since moral beliefs are usually emotionally toned, such an approach may also impede any objective analysis of a firm's actual progress in the area of merit employment. When managements view integration primarily as a moral problem, they frequently seem to feel they need only convince their employees that integration is "right" to bring it about. Talk alone, however, is seldom effective. While a few people might admit their dislike for Negroes, many people find it difficult to become fully cognizant of their own prejudices, and discrimination can be continued in practice without the conscious intent of either employees or management. A case in point is the personnel manager who found that one of his subordinates had unintentionally discouraged many Negroes from accepting employment with the company simply by failing to explain to them, in the same detail as he had done for whites, the opportunities for future advancement.

Similarly, managements adopting the "moral" approach to integration often tend to gear their efforts to those of their competitors. Because of this, they frequently become extremely touchy when accused of not doing enough, since by all visible signs they are certainly

doing as much as anyone else. Not yet seeing integration as a pragmatic necessity closely related to profit and loss and, therefore, not
approaching it with the proper thought and careful research, companies assuming the moral tactic often find themselves in contradictory and uncomfortable positions. The president of one boycotted
company, for example, said that he now felt morally obligated to resist Negro pressures since negotiation would be tantamount to an admission of guilt. On the other hand, he also admitted that he and his
competitors had not done all they might to encourage integration.
Again, the moral approach to integration strongly suggests the need
for a personal rather than an institutional solution to the problem.
This tends to cover up management's generally vast unfamiliarity
with the basic problems surrounding the Negro: where and how he
lives and the kinds of training and information he needs to gain.

As one alternative to a moralistic stance, one vice-president suggested that a more workable criterion for integration decisions might
be the "functional" approach. He emphasized pragmatic reasons for
integrating. As a businessman, he felt that he had neither the inclination nor the ability to alter social trends. Instead, he felt responsible,
regardless of his personal beliefs, for preparing his company for
what he considered to be inevitable change. While he recognized an
opportunity for those companies to practice aggressive business
leadership in the realm of civil rights, he felt that altruistic policies
were generally out of place in the business environment. Yet, at the
same time, he believed that much of the opportunity for integration by
choice had passed, and that most companies would now integrate out
of necessity. This necessity, he concluded, was a fact with which companies could no longer argue; of which, at worst, they could only be
unaware.

# — 2

# INITIATING THE CORPORATE POLICY

Today most organizations have a written policy proclaiming equal employment opportunity for all, in all job categories. By themselves, however, these written policies are relatively ineffectual.

First, a few misleading theories about Negroes are often held by people in supervisory and management positions. One of these claims that "customers will not accept Negroes in certain jobs." Another is that "the productivity of the white workers will decrease if they are forced to work alongside Negroes." Also, "Negroes are just not dependable." In most companies these theories remain untested. Where they _have_ been tested, they have proved unjust. An illustration can be found in the experience of a small mid-western dairy, which obtained a large portion of its revenues through home delivery salesmen. These salesmen had frequent contact with customers and, in some cases, even had keys to customers' houses so they could put the milk in the refrigerator when no one was home. Because of this customer-salesman relationship, the sales manager was afraid to place a Negro in one of these positions. It was only at top management insistence that the sales manager hired several Negroes. In fact, in order to get him to make this move, top management agreed not to hold him responsible for any loss in sales attributable to Negro route salesmen. The sales

12

manager received a pleasant surprise, however. Instead of declining, sales actually increased on the Negroes' routes and several adjacent routes. There appeared to be two reasons. First, the Negroes were conscientious workers and extremely polite and friendly. Apparently even more important, most customers were pleased to see Negroes being given this opportunity. Several letters received by the company from new white customers testified to the fact that these new accounts were filed in appreciation of the company's integration efforts.

The above is just one of several examples, but it illustrates an important point. Because of untested and unproven theories, supervisory personnel, especially those involved in hiring, quite frequently are unwilling to accept the perceived risk of hiring a Negro.

A second reason why a written equal employment opportunity policy is insufficient by itself lies in the behavior pattern of the Negro communities. The Negro generally has not seen an opportunity for himself in industry. The result in the past has been that the majority of those qualified Negroes who had the ambition and financial means to attend college prepared themselves for professions such as medicine, law, education, and social work, where they knew they could make use of their college experience. Not only were they not preparing themselves for careers in industry, but they were often completely uninterested in even applying for such jobs. Negroes have been turned down so frequently in the past that they just expect to be turned down again if they apply. Hence, many Negroes generally will not appear voluntarily at the employment office.

If management personnel are unwilling to take the risk of hiring an equally qualified Negro, and if many qualified Negroes will not seek employment of their own accord, it seems quite clear that a written equal employment opportunity policy alone is bound to be unrealistic and ineffective.

## Necessity of Support at the Top

What is required is a working policy that has the unqualified support of the top man in the organization. This man must understand the situation that exists today and furnish the leadership necessary to make the written equal employment opportunity policies a reality. If his support is clear, and his leadership strong, management will be inclined to take the perceived risks it has avoided in the past, and Negroes will begin to see real opportunities behind the employment office door.

A statement made by Labor Secretary Willard Wirtz, while addressing a conference of 63 corporation presidents who had been invited to join the Plans for Progress, stresses the need for the top man's commitment, "The question of whether the principle of human dignity does or does not control within any organization depends on one thing, and that is whether you, the men at the top, can say this is the way this is going to be."*

The extent of the top executive's commitment in any organization will usually be quite apparent. Interviews with two international companies in the same industry illustrate the varying degrees to which this commitment can go. Both firms have similar types of operation and both are signatories of the Plans for Progress.

In Company A, it is readily apparent that the president has committed his organization to an active integration program, and notable results have been achieved. Negroes have been brought into the firm at several levels. A number of Negroes who formerly held low-level positions have been upgraded through participation in a "skilled trade" training program. Most practices of segregation have been removed from the plants. Because of these changes, Negroes are now convinced that opportunity does exist for them in the organization, and the number of qualified Negroes applying for jobs has increased.

In Company B, it is apparent that the president has only been paying lip service to the Plans for Progress, and his lack of enthusiasm has permeated the entire management structure. The general feeling of the people with whom we spoke was that they hoped the whole movement would slow down—"It's just going too fast." On the whole, Com-

---

*From an address made in the East Room of the White House on January 16, 1964.

14

pany B accomplished little. Entire factories are still segregated to the extent that a brick wall separates the white and Negro workers. Every Negro applicant is still required to be over-qualified for the job for which he is being considered. Further research into the attitude of the president of this firm indicates that he personally is not committed to the ideals behind the Plans for Progress.

On the basis of several interviews with organizations similar to Company B, it seems fair to conclude that unless the president pledges his firm allegiance to the policy of equal employment opportunity, others within the organization cannot effectively implement such a policy. As with any other major operating policy, top management leadership and interest is absolutely essential.

## A Method for Establishing the Required Support

Developing the framework for a viable integration program can be thought of as a four-step process. First, it is essential that top management conduct a careful examination of the existing practices being followed by the various members of the organization. Second, the high-level decisions regarding the intended involvement of the company in a program of this nature must be translated into an explicit set of goals. Third, the policy must be communicated to all levels of the organization. Fourth, a control system must be established for measuring the performance of everyone involved in applying the policy.

A careful internal analysis should enable top management to gain insight into any subtle discrimination which presently exists. Such insight will be essential in developing effective techniques for measuring the company's progress. And, it will indicate to a great extent what company executives can hope to accomplish with their equal employment opportunity program. This self-examination should include a scrutiny of the composition of the present work force, with particular emphasis on Negro employees.

   1. How many Negro employees are there?
   2. What positions do they now hold?

3. Are these positions considered to be strictly "Negro jobs?"
4. How were these men hired?
5. Are these Negroes treated differently from whites?
6. Do they use the same facilities?
7. Exactly what are their skills?
8. Are they promotable?
9. Have they been considered for any promotions?
10. Have they received promotions commensurate with their ability?
11. Do they really have the same opportunity?
12. What is their attitude toward the company?

Honest answers to questions such as these should clearly indicate what the situation is today.

In order to determine what changes with respect to equal employment opportunity can be made in the future, it is necessary to know just how the total work force will change. How fast is it expected to grow? What skills will be required? What skills will no longer be required? What sort of promotion opportunities will be feasible? What is the turnover rate expected to be? For what jobs will it be necessary to hire only skilled men? How will it be possible for these men to acquire these skills? For what skills will the company choose, or be forced, to train its present employees? For what skills will it be essential to train new men? What qualifications should a new employee be required to have? Are all of these qualifications relevant to the job? How will applicants be tested to determine the extent to which they possess these qualifications?

These are all very general questions, but they should be asked of each specific type of work in every plant and office location. This detail is particularly essential in a multi-location, multi-product company, if the answers are to be of any value. When a detailed analysis such as this is supplemented by an examination of the external environment for each plant location, it becomes possible to estimate how much a company can conceivably accomplish in a given period of time. A study of the environment should consider, among other things, the following questions: What minority groups are located within the company's employment area? What percentage of the community work force do they represent? What skills do they now have? At what rate are they attaining skills that will be useful to the company in the future? If the answers to these questions are unsatisfactory, what can be done to improve the situation?

One additional factor should be evaluated in the process of determining what a company can <u>realistically</u> accomplish over a given period of time. Essentially, this concerns the amount of pressure that can be put on the present organization to force its integration. The extent to which pressure can be applied is a function of the commitment of individual employees to the organization, a factor which varies widely among industries and companies. Consider the application of this criterion to two industries.

In Industry A, most employees expect their company to provide them with long-term employment and security. Quite frequently these people have started at lower salaries than they could have obtained in other industries because they were willing to sacrifice starting salary for long-term security. These people are usually strongly committed to the company and are not likely to consider leaving if they should initially disagree with a new company policy.

On the other hand, in Industry B, many employees feel little commitment to any particular company. Instead, their commitment is to the industry as a whole or to their own profession. Men in this field change jobs rather frequently, and often on only slight provocation. It seems apparent that top management could afford to be considerably more dictatorial regarding corporate policy in Industry A than in Industry B.

The nature of the industry is only one factor that affects employees' commitment to a company. Other factors include the age of employees, their years of company service, their perceived advancement opportunity, and the supply of men with comparable skills available in the labor market. In essence, executives should consider the commitment of their employees when determining how fast to proceed with integration efforts. Mention of this factor of commitment may imply that an integration effort places considerable strain on the management-employee relationship. It is not at all necessary that this be the case. As Chapter 6 points out in some detail, many of the problems anticipated by companies at the outset of a program never materialized at all.

However, even imagined problems can disrupt an organization if they are not taken into consideration. The more the employees are committed to the company and its goals, the more willing they will be to follow top management's leadership. On the other hand, where the employee commitment is not strong, the perceived problems may cause employees to seek alternatives other than those proposed by the leaders of the organization. In such a situation, company officers may have to use a milder program to bring everyone along. Fortunately, however, employees are much more receptive to this movement now than they were even a few years ago.

An analysis such as has been described should help management to develop a realistic program to be discussed in later chapters for the integration of the organization. As with most other management programs, it will be necessary to establish working goals for several future points in time.

A number of companies favor the use of target goals similar to those utilized in other operating programs. If used, such target goals should be based on population concentrations adjusted for anticipated fluctuations, and should be broken down by plant locations and types of skills to account for the many different situations that exist. Such goals should only be used as rough guidelines, and should never be enforced to the point where their attainment becomes the essential task of operating personnel. In addition, considerable caution must be exercised in the overt usage of goals even as general guidelines, since civil rights groups may trap management in an inflexible and unreasonable position if management resorts publicly to the numbers game.

Once a positive decision has been made to proceed with an active platform, there are numerous ways, some of which are discussed below, in which company leaders can emphasize the depth of their intentions.

Joining the Plans for Progress provided an effective media for many large companies. The signing of the Plans by the president or the chief executive officer usually received enough publicity in national, state, local and company press to make it abundantly clear that the organization's executives were fully committed. Most of these companies followed up this publicity by distributing copies of the company's own plan for progress throughout the organization. In some cases, all employees received a copy; in others, distribution was restricted to salaried personnel.

Some of the smaller companies were able to join state and local programs very much like the national Plans for Progress and gain similar publicity. Others preferred to develop their own plan, which they distributed among employees. A third group simply restated or reintroduced their existing equal opportunity policy, making it very clear that it was to be followed.

Frequently, the president of a firm would speak to large groups of management personnel. In certain companies, the president made an effort to personally visit every plant location and speak. In other organizations, he would appoint a personnel assistant to do this very same thing—emphasizing that this man was his personal representative.

These speeches appeared to be very effective for two reasons. First, they showed that the program had the president's support. Second, they usually told the employees why the company had committed itself to such a program. This gave the employees a chance to develop their own thinking as to why their participation in such a program was necessary.

In several organizations, members of top management became extremely active in external affairs to make it obvious that they endorsed programs for the advancement of minority groups. Some made speeches to Negro groups and became active in such associations as the Urban League. Others sponsored training programs in cooperation with other corporations. These are some of the most common methods found for conveying the organization's commitment to its equal employment opportunity policy.

Although the foregoing practices facilitate the effective introduction of a company's policy, the initial momentum so gained will not carry the program for very long. The maintenance of proper implementation in the long term requires the establishment of a permanent procedure for generating continual feedback to top management. This process of upward communication serves a two-fold purpose: 1) it keeps company executives informed of possible problem areas; 2) it is a constant reminder to operating people that the firm's leaders are closely following the actual implementation of corporate policy. Regular reports that originate at local personnel offices best meet both of these criteria. Experience thus far seems to indicate that the most useful reports stress the accomplishment during the reporting period rather than total progress to date. Some of the types of information to be included in these reports might be:

1. The number of job openings occurring during the period.
2. The number of Negroes interviewed.
3. The number of Negroes interviewed as a percentage of the total number of applicants hired.
4. The number of Negroes hired.
5. The number of Negroes hired as a percentage of the total number of applicants hired.
6. The number of Negroes promoted or upgraded.
7. The number of Negroes trained for specific skills.

All data could be subdivided by localities and meaningful skill categories.

It is also helpful if these reports contain space for including details of local programs. Such details might include a description of division participation in a high-school career day, an account of recruiting efforts, or a summary of the status of a developing training program. Including this type of information allows a division manager to report on precisely what he is doing, as well as on the demonstrable effects on his work force.

In the beginning, it may be best to require these reports every three to four months. Later, perhaps, the frequency can be reduced to every six months. Reporting more frequently than every three months is apt to put too much pressure on the organization and cause responses purely for the sake of reporting. Precisely this type of situation occurred in the recent experience of a large concern having sales offices throughout the United States. A great deal of pressure was placed on each of these offices to meet rather ambitious monthly sales quotas. Since the reporting system was built around these sales quotas, most of the reports were on a monthly basis. Therefore, when members of top management started requesting integration reports, they put these on the same basis.

Having this report come due at the same time and with the same regularity as the monthly sales reports simply applied too much additional pressure to some of the sales managers. It soon became apparent that several managers were hiring the first Negro that came in the door in an attempt to make their reports look good, while at the same time taking as little time as possible away from the more pressing problem of meeting their sales quota. The results were bound to be unfavorable. Not only did this quickly tend to create the impression among local Negroes that the company's actions were strictly for show, but it increased the likelihood that antagonistic feelings would develop within the branch. The Negro might be overqualified, in which case he would probably soon become frustrated and leave, or he might well be a gold brick whose presence would tend to cause resentment among the white employees. Their resentment would almost inevitably be directed at the home office management, on the reasoning that it was management's new policy which had led to the pressure to hire an unqualified Negro.

We also found several examples of the other extreme where the reports were too infrequent to serve as a reminder of the company's commitment. One such example concerned a company which was one of the early signatories of the Plans for Progress, and which had developed its internal integration reporting schedule to match that required by the Plans. This schedule demands several reports during the first year, followed by annual reports in subsequent years. Partially as a result of relying on this reporting schedule, the company's efforts were not effective across-the-board; and by the end of the second year, relatively little was actually being accomplished, except in those larger locations which were being visited regularly by its personnel auditors. At this point, the company developed a "Plans for Progress Checklist" which every division was required to file on a more frequent basis. This checklist succeeded in rejuvenating the division's thinking in the desired manner. A copy of the checklist appears on the following pages. It should be examined closely, as it provides an excellent example of an effective supplementary report to be used in conjunction with the employment and interviewing figures.

It is impossible to prescribe specific rules for the format and frequency of these performance reports. The characteristics of the business and the desired results should dictate the most appropriate reporting procedure in any particular case. It is essential that some regularized system be adopted, however, if the desired activity and direction of a company's integration program is to be preserved. It must be carefully planned and regularly reviewed. If this is done, it can be a most effective method of keeping a company's integration effort active and moving in the right direction.

# PLAN FOR PROGRESS CHECKLIST

<u>Note</u>: Comments should be recorded for <u>every</u> question. If the answer to the question is "Yes," then the comment should describe the nature of the action which was taken. If the answer is "No," the comment should give the reason the action has not been taken and/or the nature of the action which is planned.

<u>General</u>

1. Has <u>recent</u> action been taken to insure that <u>all</u> management employees are conversant with the company's Plan for Progress and our obligation thereunder?     Yes_____ No_____

   Comments: _____

   _____

   _____

2. Has <u>recent</u> action been taken to insure that all employees are aware of our non-discriminating policy?     Yes_____ No_____

   Comments: _____

   _____

   _____

3. Have the local unions, if any, and their current officers been informed of the company's Plan for Progress and the affirmative actions we are required to take thereunder?     Yes_____ No_____

   Comments: _____

   _____

   _____

4. Have appropriate posters been placed on bulletin boards in accordance with the regulations?     Yes_____ No_____

   Comments: _____

   _____

General (Cont.)

    5.  When your location advertises for em-
ployees, does such employment advertising include the phrase, "An Equal Opportunity Employer"?                 Yes_____ No_____

        Comments: _____

_____

_____

## Notification

    1.  Have all public and private recruitment
sources normally used at the location
been advised in writing within the past
year that the company is an equal opportunity employer?                 Yes_____ No_____

        Comments: _____

_____

_____

    2.  Have high schools and colleges in the im-
mediate area having substantial numbers
of non-white students been notified in writing within the past year that the company
is an equal opportunity employer?     Yes_____No_____

        Comments: _____

_____

_____

## Recruitment

    1.  Have positive steps been taken to develop
and maintain sources of recruitment which
will increase the number of qualified non-
white applicants?                Yes_____ No_____

        Comments: _____

_____

_____

2. Have active working relationships been established and maintained with the local non-white community through the medium of the Urban League or other similar community groups?                    Yes_____ No_____

   Comments: _____

   _____

   _____

3. In the case of plant locations, have active working relationships been established and maintained with the principals and vocational counselors of nearby high schools having substantial numbers of non-white students?                    Yes_____ No_____

   Comments: _____

   _____

   _____

Employment

1. Have all employment application and other employment forms and records been reviewed to insure that no reference to race, creed, color, or national origin exists?          Yes_____No_____

   Comments: _____

   _____

   _____

2. Have objective criteria for making hiring and upgrading decisions, such as written job requirements, aptitude tests, etc., been established to the maximum extent practical?                    Yes_____ No_____

   Comments: _____

   _____

   _____

Employment (Cont.)

3. Do application and employment files contain sufficient information to insure adequate support for employment and upgrading decisions?           Yes_____No_____

   Comments: _____

   _____

   _____


Miscellaneous

1. Is the company's Plan for Progress reviewed periodically at staff meetings at various levels of the organization?           Yes_____No_____

   Comments:_____

   _____

   _____


2. Is the company's Plan for Progress included in the content of supervisory training programs?           Yes_____No_____

   Comments: _____

   _____

   _____


3. Have steps been taken to recognize and publicize outstanding accomplishments of employees who are minority group members?           Yes_____ No_____

   Comments: _____

   _____

   _____

Miscellaneous (Cont.)

4.  Have arrangements been made to docu-
    ment the affirmative actions which have
    been taken in accordance with the provi-
    sions of the company's Plan for Progress? Yes_____No_____

    Comments: _____

    _____

    _____

5.  Are company facilities maintained, except
    where otherwise legally required, on a
    non-segregated basis?                    Yes_____ No_____

    Comments: _____

    _____

    _____

Location _____      Signed_____

Number of Employees_____        Title_____
  Covered by Checklist

# — 3

# BUILDING CONSTRUCTIVE RELATIONS
# WITH NEGRO GROUPS

Traditionally there has been little contact between the business world and the Negro community, and the lack of communication has produced a wide gulf of misunderstanding. With civil rights pressures in various forms being experienced everywhere, the business world is being forced to recognize and deal with this national problem. There are many cases in which companies have taken the lead in integration, but such cases have been all too few, basically because integration has been a problem for which business has not felt responsible. Therefore, there has been little reason to resolve the problem at the company level.

The purpose of this chapter is to discuss possible methods of establishing the foundation for a workable process of integrating a business, both at the hourly and the salaried levels. This foundation consists of an understanding of the forces at work in the Negro community and a meaningful and profitable relationship developed with this community.

## *Direct Personal Contact with Negro Organizations*

Perhaps the most fruitful way to begin to develop an appreciation for the Negro's situation is to communicate personally with the various leaders of all the influential groups in the Negro community. Without this kind of personal contact, it is extremely difficult to understand the motivations and actions of the various Negro groups. This is not to say it is impossible; in fact, several companies included in this study have carried out successful programs without following this step. But in every case, the man who is directing the company's integration efforts has a much higher than average understanding of the Negro community, and is successful in communicating this understanding to the other employees involved. Few companies have men who already possess this awareness and, therefore, they must encourage development of this capacity if an understanding is to be gained.

The value of such men can be seen in the case of a company that had been visited twice by representatives of a Negro action group, who were demanding that the company recruit actively and hire more Negro men for placement in more responsible positions. Having previously signed the Plans for Progress, the executives of the company felt they were doing their share. However, being somewhat disturbed by the prospect of economic reprisal, and also realizing that they were really not giving Negroes entirely equal treatment, they assigned a personnel man the task of developing a recruiting and hiring program for the Negro community. After studying the situation, the man moved into the largest Negro section of the city for the summer. The understanding he developed during this period has since enabled him to develop a program which has gained his organization a solid reputation and a loyal clientele within the Negro community. There is now little possibility of harassment of this company by Negro groups.

Some of the measures this man formulated included the following: a revision of the use and evaluation of aptitude tests; a review of personnel interviewers to ensure equal treatment; a recruiting campaign within the Negro community; a better understanding throughout the company of the Negro problem; and an awareness among the employees as to the reasons why the company was taking such an active role in searching for solutions. It is significant to note that the company's white customers have not shown any inclination to protest the above measures.

Admittedly, living in the Negro community for three months is an extreme method of developing contact. However, it seems quite likely that without this man's thorough understanding of Negro problems the progressive measures outlined above would probably not have been developed. Because he understood the forces and the people of the Negro community, the personnel man was able to effect proposals which would avoid possible areas of conflict.

There are other reasons for initiating contact with the Negro community. One of the most important considerations is the supply of applicants Negro leaders might direct to a given company. (This subject will be further discussed in Chapter 4.) A second reason is that contact establishes a company's reputation for "fair play" within the Negro community and thereby gains a larger market for the firm's products or services. But the most important reason for establishing a relationship is the risk involved in not doing so. Without direct contact, a company cannot fully understand the Negro's attitudes and actions and will probably be poorly prepared to deal with them.

Contact with Negro leaders should be developed even by integrated companies in order to demonstrate the sincerity of their effort and maintain their reputation within the Negro community. Having Negroes in a company's work force is no guarantee that it will not be faced with economic or physical harassment. Often, a company which was matching the integration programs of other firms in the same indus-try and city has been confronted with a boycott or a picket line. For example, a food supplier had employed Negroes in its production facilities for many years and would have considered them for sales routes had any applied. The firm also had the largest market share in the Negro community, but the management lacked an awareness of Negroes' desires and had no contact with Negro leaders. As a result it sustained a boycott which resulted in a sizeable loss of sales, profits, and community respect.

In another case, a financial institution servicing more Negroes than any other in its city became the object of picketing and sit-in demonstrations because it had failed to comprehend the nature and extent of the Negroes' employment demands. Seriously underestimating the methods and capabilities of the local Negro leaders, this company had attempted to avoid direct contact with them.

In several instances, a company's initiation of a working relationship prevented a disturbance, probably a boycott, at some later date. Management of a consumer goods company, for instance, decided entirely of its own volition to undertake a more active program of recruitment and training. This program was developed to alleviate certain conditions discovered through contact with two or three Negro groups. It was a success, and an excellent working relationship resulted. A year later when a Negro action group was boycotting a similar firm, its leader remarked that if the company had not undertaken this program it, rather than its competitor, would probably have been the target of the boycott.

It should be clear that building a relationship with the Negro community is a lot less costly than ignoring it. The company can expect to receive additional applicants, avoid harassment, demonstrate social responsibility, and, most important, gain insight into the integration movement. Having made this contact, a company will find that the Negro community is anxious to reciprocate. So far, its leaders have been approached by very few companies which have a genuine interest in generating cooperation and understanding, and are sincerely interested in the Negro cause, rather than merely in their own personal betterment. Most leaders are, therefore, eager to work with any company which approaches them to establish an atmosphere of trust. As an example, the man described above who lived in the Negro community is currently considered to be a real friend by the Negro leaders in his locale. They tend to direct promising Negro applicants to his company first. Moreover, they trust him and respect his answers to their requests, whereas they might immediately distrust the same answers from someone less familiar to them.

Once the basic reasons for developing a relationship have been clarified, it is necessary to consider with whom contact should be made and how it should be made. A common question is "Who speaks for the Negro community?" Obviously, no one individual or group does, and it is highly improbable that any single representative ever will. There is a political spectrum within the Negro community just as surely as there are Republicans and Democrats and the various degrees of liberalism and conservatism within those two broad class-ifications. Just as the leaders of a corporation must understand or at least have a working knowledge of the two political parties if they are to operate effectively in varying political climates, so they must understand the viewpoints and policies of the various Negro groups in order to conduct a successful integration program.

As most companies recognize, there are five Negro organizations at the national level which carry sufficient weight within the Negro community to gain national publicity. From left to right in terms of tactics utilized, speed of integration desired, and political philosophy, but not in terms of red, pink or "true blue" they are: the Student Non-Violent Coordinating Committee (SNCC); the Congress of Racial Equality (CORE); the National Association for the Advancement of Colored People (NAACP); and the Urban League. The fifth group is the Black Muslims, whose credo of racial separation makes them difficult to classify among integration groups, but whose militant posture demands that their potential be recognized. One Southern group, the Southern Christian Leadership Conference, headed by Dr. Martin Luther King, Jr., also deserves mention in view of its frequent demonstrations for equal treatment that often receive national publicity.

However, in many cities the most powerful organizations are not the local branches of the national organizations, but such ad hoc groups as the Philadelphia Ministerial Alliance or the Boston Action Group. These groups arise to sponsor spontaneous demonstrations and are unfettered by national constitutions. They very quickly become a strong voice in the community because of their ability to act quickly, because the leaders remain close to the Negro populace, and because these leaders are usually excellent organizers. Sometimes, the leaders of these local action groups are the branch officers of national organizations who have seen the necessity for action more rapid than that permitted by the restrictive constitutions of such groups as the NAACP or CORE. Usually, however, the leaders seem to rise from the masses. They are frequently at the forefront of civil rights demonstrations.

There are several ways to determine who the real powers are. The most direct method is to observe the leaders and organizers of local demonstrations. Another way to locate the leaders is through the local chapters of the national organizations. Herein lies another good reason for establishing contact with all groups: it is a direct way to find out where the real strength lies.

Actually, the easiest method whereby a company can determine the locus of power within the Negro community is to contact other companies which have had more experience in the integration area. Utilizing and sharing common experiences cannot be stressed too greatly, for it is almost a certainty that the Negroes a specific company deals with have dealt with other businesses before. And their backlog of experience enables them to anticipate the company's answers and strategy, perhaps even before the company itself has fully defined them. Therefore, knowledge of the experience of other firms is valuable.

### Attitudes of Various Negro Organizations

One important determinant of contact with Negro organizations is a familiarity with the attitudes of these groups toward each other and toward companies whose contacts may be restricted to particular Negro groups.

As one moves to the left on the organizational spectrum described above, there is a growing degree of intolerance for what seems to be the inaction of the groups to the right. But, as one moves to the right, each group seems to believe in the goals of those to the left, and to disagree only on the means of achieving those goals. Representatives of even the most conservative organizations, however, admit that the tactics used by direct action groups serve a useful purpose. Although the officers of the more conventional civil rights groups generally abhor the principles of the Black Muslims, the Muslim movement has a certain appeal among the lower echelons and the broad base of the

Negro populace. This appeal could grow in intensity if a working relationship is not established with the more conventional groups by a responsible white community.

The Urban League is the group with which the majority of business-men prefer to deal, primarily because its basic beliefs and practices appear more similar to those of most companies than other Negro groups. And as an obvious corollary, the League appears to have less appeal to the average Negro than do other organizations. It does not participate in such direct actions as picketing or boycotting. On the contrary, it advocates a moderate approach to integration which will minimize hard feelings on both sides. In most cases it is the best available source of qualified Negroes other than a company's own direct recruiting, and it can provide excellent advice on pilot placements and general absorption. (The Skills Bank and pilot placement concepts are discussed in Chapters 4 and 6.) Because of the quality of Negro applicants it can offer, and the extensive experience of its leaders, the Urban League should be contacted and supported.

But the League is usually not enough. In fact, our research indicates that if a company deals only with the League it can be inviting major problems both from within the company and from outside sources. Because of the League's policy of moderation and its reluctance to adopt "direct action" practices, it has lost a significant amount of its appeal to the Negro, particularly in the younger age groups and basic laboring class. Several Negroes interviewed said that the League is looked upon as charity, the place where a Negro goes when he is "really down" and cannot find a job. It should be emphasized, however, that, as is the case with most of the other Negro organizations, the reputation and effectiveness of the League in any particular area depends considerably on the caliber and personality of its local leadership.

This image among many members of the Negro community has brought the charge of "Uncle Tomism" against the League. The accusation is unfortunate, for in the long run the League could be a better liaison between industry and the Negro community than any other group. It is the place to which other organizations turn when they are confronted with the inevitable question: "Where can we find qualified Negroes?" The League is given credit by the various Negro groups for this service. Because of its conservative image, a company which deals exclusively with the League invites problems from the members of other associations, who, believing that such limited contact is only a smoke screen to camouflage a lack of action on the real problem, will not allow a company to proceed on this basis. It might be said, then, that by dealing only with the League, a company does not get a true picture of the Negro community; it gets only the most conservative and diluted version of the feelings and demands that exist. Therefore contact with additional groups is recommended.

The NAACP, as it affects the business community, is basically designed to stimulate and force legal action on such questions as union apprentice restrictions and the enactment of Fair Employment Practice legislation. It also participates in some direct action protests, but its locals are somewhat restricted in this regard by their national constitutions. This restriction has caused many NAACP officers to assist in the development of ad hoc action committees. Most of these local officers sincerely believe that direct action is the road they must take for two reasons: 1) it is most effective in dealing with specific companies; 2) it has the greatest appeal to the Negro community. It is important to realize and understand considerations of this sort. Just as a company must understand the political structure of its unions, it must be aware of the political factors which affect the bargaining units of the Negro community.

The NAACP is probably the most conservative of the direct action groups, but it is being forced to take a more militant stand because of the growth of CORE and various local action associations. It seems likely that the NAACP organization, as well as its various local leaders, will become more militant in the near future and participate in more direct action maneuvers. It is also quite possible that the NAACP, because of its long and well-known history, could become the focus of, or at least a strong participant in, a national coordinating body. The purpose of such a body would be to carry out the planning and leadership of regional or even national direct actions such as the boycott of a chain of food stores, or the picketing of a multi-plant corporation. In summary, it can be said that the NAACP is generally a dependable group with which to work, and, due to its long history, still remains the most potent force in the Negro community.

The philosophies and methods of CORE, SNCC, and the ad hoc action committees are very similar. They have all been formed to bring economic and socio-political pressure to bear on any institution which they feel is discriminatory, and against which they can develop sufficient support to maintain a sustained drive. They have a strong appeal within the community because they demand things immediately; in several cases their street-side demonstrations have achieved substantial gains. But normally they have nothing to offer a company in the way of guidance or prospective job candidates.

Their method of operation is looked upon with much disfavor by industry in general and perhaps by more conservative Negro groups. A company's normal reaction is either to assert that no external body is going to dictate its hiring practices, or to demand that the protesting group come to its own assistance by supplying some Negroes which the company could hire. Immediately, constructive communication between the two groups is denied, and the battle lines are drawn.

A working relationship built on personal contact with the leaders of these direct action groups should avoid such communication breakdowns. Through such contact, the top managers of a company can begin to understand the reasons why demonstrations are carried out in their customary manner; they can begin to locate the real seats of power; and, most importantly, whites and Negroes can begin to work together to alleviate the integration problem. Whether the majority of the problems in a specific company are real or imaginary makes little difference if the company has not made its situation clear to the various Negro leaders before it is confronted with a series of demands. An unnecessary battle may be waged; a chance to work constructively toward a solution may be passed by. Once the battle begins, profits will suffer for four reasons: the obvious loss of Negro sales; the possible loss of other sales to Negro sympathizers or people who simply seek to avoid disturbances; loss of executive time diverted to unprofit-

36

able pursuits; and, in most cases, losses due to hurried hiring for positions which could have been better filled in a more leisurely, rational atmosphere.

To obtain the maximum amount of information, and to insure that a company is reaching the powers-that-be within the Negro community, contact with all groups, no matter how disagreeable their tactics, is desirable.

## Methods of Establishing Contact

The method of contacting Negroes is extremely important, and requires the consideration of several factors. Perhaps the most significant fact to be realized is that the Negroes to be dealt with are leaders of a substantial group of people. They are recognized within their own community as the most influential people in it. The Negro leaders are to their people as the mayor or corporate executive is to the white community; as such they feel they are entitled to the same treatment given to a white civic leader. For the company-Negro relationship to attain any degree of success these men must know their position is respected. Some business executives may feel that the Negro leader has not yet earned the right to demand their time. But, as noted earlier, the problem is so significant that the time and attention of a top official is a wise and sound investment. The impact upon the Negro leader of an initial contact and a demonstration of genuine interest by a company director is considerable. The Negro leader immediately knows that his position is respected and that the company really intends to solve the problem. After a proper foundation is laid, the need for contact between top management and the Negro leaders diminishes. The responsibility for maintaining the relationship on a day-to-day basis shifts to the personnel office, with only a periodic need for demonstrations of interest by upper management.

## Possible Locations for Initial Contacts

The initial meeting might be held in the top manager's office or regular conference room. After an investigation by the personnel office as to which Negro leaders should be invited—based, of course, on the degree of influence they wield in the Negro community rather than on the "whiteness" of their attitude—a personal invitation by the president or general manager is an effective way to begin. A meeting at the company's, rather than the Negroes', offices seems to make a better impression because it shows that top executives are perfectly willing to let company personnel know they are actively seeking solutions. One Negro leader offered this comment: "The president, some of the board members, and maybe the personnel director—now there's my idea of a good meeting." Only by a demonstration of concern at this level could the company have succeeded in convincing this Negro of its genuine interest in working with him to solve the integration issues.

Other methods for continuing to show interest at the highest level would include attendance at luncheons or meetings conducted by the Negro groups, not organizational meetings, but, for instance, luncheons held from time to time by the NAACP to stimulate contact among various business, social, political and Negro leaders. A company could also work with civic projects which concern the Negro movement. Participation of this type will help the company's executives to better understand the issues involved and help the Negroes to understand the difficulties facing industry.

### Negroes' Knowledge of Business

Negro leaders involved in the civil rights movement frequently have a rather incomplete idea of how a business operates. Many know only that there are executives, managers, foremen, and laborers, and very few have any real grasp of the responsibilities of the business executive. They must be exposed to the functioning of a business if they are to understand its problems. They do not realize that a company considers certain information—data on salaries, for instance—to be proprietary, or why. In many cases they feel they are being snubbed when they are summarily refused such information instead of being given ranges for various job classifications and told why specific salaries cannot be revealed.

The value of showing the Negro leaders how a business works and how an industry functions cannot be overemphasized as an integral part of the relationship a company wishes to build. In passing on information concerning a business, one thing in particular should be borne in mind: the Negro is seeking status as well as economic equality. He does not believe that Negro jobs stop at the foreman level. Therefore the company should be particularly careful to explain its managerial functions.

## Attitudes to Expect from Negro Leaders

These considerations are especially important when Negro representatives make the first approach. The Negro leaders must be treated with the respect their position commands in their community, and assisted in understanding the functions of the company. The local leaders will probably be very mannerly in the company office, but in many cases, they may lack the sophistication to which the company officers are accustomed. It is unreasonable to expect them to act otherwise, since they have had little, if any, exposure to the business environment. A word of caution is appropriate at this point, however. On the specific issue of company-Negro contact and negotiation, the Negro leaders will probably be more sophisticated and knowledgeable than anyone in the company. The company must realize that the Negroes have been through the process of company contact, threats, pickets, boycotts, and working relationship before. The company, on the other hand, probably has not. If it had, the Negro leaders would probably not be there.

The Negro leaders have learned their trade well. Moreover, their sophistication and organizational capability has been increasing rapidly. It can be assumed, therefore, that they have carefully developed their plans before approaching the company. And, if negotiations falter, the plans will usually include a provision for active retaliation. As time goes by, picketing demonstrations are increasingly likely to be noisy and unrestrained. Such demonstrations attract more participants; more important, Negroes have found that they get faster action. A company embarrassed by groups of chanting marchers undertakes action much more quickly than one confronted by silent pickets. The showy demonstration is a tactic which the Negroes are forced to use to get adequate support and immediate action. Because of this, company executives should not be surprised if the Negro leader and his supporters seem to be acting unreasonably. Instead of holding these tactics against the Negroes, management must realize that they are a part of the total package to be dealt with.

In conclusion, it should be remembered that Negro leaders believe integration to be the concern of top management, a category in which they frequently do not include the head of the personnel department. Hence it may well be advisable for the president or some other top operating executive to accept the request of a particular Negro leader to meet personally with him, at least to initiate the relationship. Although in nearly all cases the Negro's demands could be handled as well or better by a personnel representative, a referral to the personnel office by the president at the outset will often suggest to the Negro that the company is not really interested in his situation. On the other hand, the Negro leader who is treated with respect and educated in the functions of the business can be a cooperative and valuable consultant and a source of better-than-average Negro personnel.

## The Use of Publicity

A number of companies have capitalized on the hiring of a few Negroes through widespread publicity in the Negro press as well as the general press. Such publicity is effective only if the company has made significant progress that is recognized within the Negro community. It is frequently a good idea to review the press statements with Negro leaders who work with the company prior to releasing them. These recommendations result from firsthand observation of the reaction of several Negro leaders to publicity of showcase hirings. No longer is the recruitment of a vice-president for the Negro market the safety valve it once was. This kind of action is now more than likely to foster immediate distrust in the Negro community.

This is not to say that a company should not make it known to the

Negro community that it is hiring Negroes. As will be explained later, it is vitally important to make it known that the company hires Negroes if more are to be attracted. But it is better, in terms of sales to Negroes and prevention of economic and physical harassment, to hire no Negroes at all than to hire one or two with the intent of publicizing the hirings in an appeal to the Negro market. Such an intent will be recognized very quickly, and an adverse reaction will occur much faster than if the company had done nothing at all.

An example of a constructive relationship in action concerns an insurance company with many offices scattered throughout the country. When one of the branch offices was threatened with a picket line by a Negro action group, the local manager defiantly produced an ancient newspaper clipping announcing the hiring of a Negro by the company. This only served to increase the vigor of the Negroes' threats. The corporate personnel man, who specialized in such problems, was summoned to deal with the group. He took the action group leaders to an integrated office some thirty miles away, promised them equal consideration in the office they were concerned with, and thereby avoided further conflict. This man's contacts with Negro groups permitted him to communicate with the people involved, and reach a solution satisfactory to both factions.

In conclusion, the following quotation from a corporate Equal Employment Opportunity Program may provide some helpful guidelines.

a) Personal contact by top management will be made with community agencies operating to facilitate equal employment opportunity for minority groups.

b) Company representatives will take part in community and corporate programs encouraging the participation of minority members in educational endeavors to increase competence and upgrade their qualifications.

A company which follows these guidelines should have a constructive, workable relationship and few, if any, integration problems.

# — 4

# DEVELOPING A RECRUITING PROGRAM

As seen by one Negro leader interviewed, the white businessman facing a local shortage of qualified Negroes has three alternative courses of action regarding the racial integration of his business. First, he can wait the six or eight years for those Negroes presently in high school to complete their secondary and college education, thereby increasing the supply of qualified Negroes. Second, he can launch an aggressive recruiting program covering large and often distant areas. Third, he can initiate an active local Negro recruiting program now, in hopes of locating Negro applicants who, while not initially able to meet the company's hiring standards, can be trained to such a level in a reasonably short period.

In the opinion of this Negro leader the first alternative is totally unacceptable to the Negro community. To the extent that a business wishes to maintain peaceful and constructive relations with the Negro community, it must adopt in some measure one or both of the others.

This attitude, common among Negroes today, is one reason why a carefully thought-out recruiting program is so crucial. The necessity for devoting some serious thought to this problem is further indicated by various comments voiced by the white business community. "Our company is willing to hire Negroes, but none seem to apply," or

42

"There just don't seem to be any Negroes in Cityville who meet our hiring standards" are two very common complaints.

Statistics indicate that if all companies were actively to seek out Negro employees, there would not be enough to satisfy the demand. However, the impression of the supply of qualified or desirable Negroes which a businessman is able to formulate on the basis of his firm's particular experience may very often underestimate the actual market supply. There is one major reason for this in a company which has not had a past policy of actively recruiting Negroes. It is simply that Negroes tend not to apply to companies which presently employ Negroes in low level jobs, in small numbers, or not at all. Unless a conscious effort is made to obtain Negro applicants this situation can easily develop over a period of years. In fact, the majority of people interviewed in this study admitted they had been very surprised to discover how applicable this description was to their own organizations when they first investigated their work force make-up and personnel experience.

Several causes may bring about such a situation. First, the primary source of information regarding applicants for employment may be existing employees. In a predominantly white company, the natural result is that very few Negroes ever get to the first level in the hiring procedure.

Second, one or more members of the personnel department may have a personal racial bias which he is allowing to act as a negative filter for any Negro applicants. The Negro can rarely overcome this obstacle, regardless of his qualifications. It is equally difficult for management to recognize and control such occurrences in a large organization, until a specific reporting system is devised and implemented.

Third, the lack of any direct effort by the company to establish contact with the Negro community will certainly reinforce the Negroes' impression that applying for a job there is a waste of time.

Increasingly, then, it will be in a company's best interest to ensure that its recruitment of Negroes is adequate, given the community and industrial environment in which it operates. This means that top management will probably find it necessary to develop a regular reporting system for checking on the implementation of recruiting policy at the operating level.

If a more aggressive, active recruiting program is required, what are some effective avenues by which to proceed? Following are some of the methods encountered in our study. The relative desirability of each will depend to some extent, of course, on factors unique to each company, and all are not essential to a successful program. However, recent experience indicates that a Negro recruiting program which does not incorporate some of them is almost certain to fail.

### Advertising—Newspapers, Magazines, and Fliers

Classified advertisements in printed media are one very common way of stimulating the inflow of prospective employees. Many companies feel that the inclusion of the phrase "An Equal Opportunity Employer" is sufficient to assure Negroes that such advertising is meant for them. In most cases, this belief is mistaken. For generations the Negro has found himself to be an implicit exception to all kinds of general rules. The experience of reading a sign stated in general terms and following its instructions, only to discover that they really referred only to whites, is all too familiar to most Negroes. It may well have been more prevalent or blatant in earlier periods, but family training and other means of direct and indirect communication have made it part of the personal or vicarious experience of today's generation. To most Negroes, therefore, the EOE stamp at the bottom of an advertisement means little and seldom provides an effective stimulus to action.

Also, most Negroes never read the want-ads appearing in the "white" dailies of the community. Their experience has taught them that it seldom pays to follow up these ads. Whether this attitude is justified by the real intentions of today's employers is neither important nor relevant. The fact remains that more direct appeals are required to convince the Negro that these opportunities are being advertised with him <u>consciously</u> in mind rather than <u>unconsciously</u> excluded.

The obvious answer is to advertise employment opportunities in the Negro press as well as the white press. In metropolitan areas, names and addresses of Negro dailies or weeklies are readily available from local offices of the Urban League, NAACP, CORE, or other knowledgeable Negro groups or individuals.* Advertising rates are frequently much lower than in the white papers, and the return in terms of Negro response is usually considerably greater.

Although a very few firms have reported little or no improvement in actual recruitment results attributable to classified advertising in Negro newspapers, there is no doubt that such advertising creates the impression that the company is sincere in its solicitation of Negro applicants. Another practice, which is closely related to the above, and which tends to reinforce its favorable effects, is the use of Negro models in the firm's normal advertising of its products or services. The process of making the initial decision to run such an advertisement has involved many hours of worry and discussion regarding its probable effect on customers, suppliers, stockholders, etc. Although the evidence available in those instances where such action was undertaken indicates the results were less adverse than had been expected, particularly where Negro models were used in ads employing several people, such factors should definitely not be minimized. An equally important point, however, and one which often does not seem to receive its fair share of consideration, is the probable effect of various courses of action on the Negro community.

Two factors appear to be involved: distribution and time. If a company wishes to use Negroes in its advertisements, but has hesitations about the effect on its total business, it may wish to "test" the idea in a Negro publication first. This is often a good approach. It at least gives the employees, stockholders, and suppliers a chance to accept

---

*For a list of Negro newspapers and Negro program radio stations, see Exhibits 2 and 3 of the Appendix.

the concept in gradual stages. In addition, it tells the Negro community that the company has at least moved off dead center and is taking positive action toward the Negro.

If the ads in Negro media are followed up within a reasonable period of time by the placement of similar ads in mixed or "white" publications, the company's image will be further strengthened in the Negro community. On the other hand, if the company continues to follow a policy of restricting advertisements utilizing Negroes to Negro publications entirely, it risks giving an impression of tokenism, which is apt to damage the company's relations with the Negro community more than if no advertising had been undertaken at all.

In brief, the situation seems to follow a general pattern. Initial advertisements utilizing Negro models but placed only in Negro publications have a positive effect at first. Long-term effects depend to a large extent on the extension of such advertising to white publications as well. The latter action goes a long way toward substantiating the sincerity of the company's commitment to conduct its business without regard to race, creed, or color. Regular advertising in Negro media maintains the very important feeling discussed above that the Negro is "consciously included" rather than "unconsciously excluded" in the firm's thinking. At no time in our study did a Negro ever say that Negroes would expect such advertising to play a dominant part in a company's advertising program.

What is true of newspaper advertising is equally true of other printed media. Among magazines, Ebony is a notable example of a good quality mass publication enjoying wide national circulation throughout the Negro community. As a source of continuing contact with events which the editors feel to be significant to the Negro community, a subscription to Ebony or a similar magazine might prove valuable to the personnel man.

A third type of printed advertising which can be used effectively is the single-sheet flier announcing information about the type of jobs available, minimum requirements for employment, and the name and address of the appropriate person to contact. These are very effective when placed on the bulletin boards at churches, community social centers, settlement houses, lodges, and public schools. Again, the element of explicit inclusion normally has favorable effects on the recruiting program.

## Local Negro Organizations

Chapter 3 described in some detail the process and importance of establishing contact with leaders of influential Negro organizations, such as the NAACP, CORE, and Urban League. These contacts can and should be utilized in the recruiting process. The rapport that each organization enjoys with the Negro community varies widely from place to place, and will have a bearing on which organization is the most productive with which to work. In any event, it does no harm for the personnel officer to keep these groups informed of the company's current personnel needs. The aid of such groups can measurably reduce the time and effort required to locate Negro applicants.

In addition to the usual broad-function groups just described, one or more organizations more specifically concerned with employment matters may exist in the community. Many New York businessmen are familiar with the Hallmark Employment Agency, an office placement agency specializing in the placement of minority group personnel. Under its owner-director, Richard "Dick" Clarke, the agency has placed more than 3,000 people "in front office positions of every type from file clerks to comptrollers."*

In Boston, an agency known as Jobs Clearing House, Inc. attempts to recruit jobless members of the Negro community, test and interview them to determine their qualifications and interests, and match these factors against a file of existing job opportunities. The owner, Tom Brown, is an experienced businessman who has established solid working relationships with most of the major firms in the area. The personnel recruiters of several Boston companies have gotten permission from their own employers to spend several hours per week of company

*New York Amsterdam News, Saturday, January 19, 1963.

time at the agency's office in order to enable Mr. Brown and his small staff to handle the flow of people. By doing this, these recruiters are developing a first-hand understanding of the Negro's problems; establishing a closer relationship with the Negro community in general and Mr. Brown in particular; and helping to maintain the quality of the processing service which the agency provides, a factor of no small importance in view of the usefulness of such a service to their own companies.

A third, and somewhat less localized employment service is sponsored by the Urban League. In late 1963, with the aid of a sizable grant from the Rockefeller Foundation, the League formed an under-employed workers' pool known as the Skills Bank. The small size of its staff, relative to the number of people who desire to avail themselves of its services, may make the Skills Bank a somewhat less thorough operation in some areas than locally established agencies such as Jobs Clearing House, Inc. Nevertheless, it should not be overlooked as a potential source of Negro applicants.

In dealing with Negro employment agencies, the company personnel recruiter should make a positive effort to reciprocate the service offered by the agency whenever the situation warrants it.

For instance, a Negro who comes to a company via an employment agency will usually return to that agency if the company does not hire him. But a Negro who comes in off the street at the suggestion of a friend will have no designated place to which to return should the company be unable to place him at the moment. He may become disillusioned at the rejection and slip quietly back into the Negro community, where locating him will prove to be a major task for some other employer. The company recruiter should make it his responsibility in such a case to contact one or more of the special agencies to help place the applicant as quickly and effectively as possible. By doing so, the recruiter will be helping the individual involved to obtain a job suited to his needs as quickly as possible, rather than allowing the Negro to conclude that this rejection is just the same old run-around he has been experiencing for years.

48

By referring the Negro to a ready job market instead of allowing him to become "lost" in the Negro community, moreover, the recruiter will be helping some other company to locate a Negro more quickly and efficiently. This can obviously be a reciprocal relationship once it is accepted practice by a group of company personnel departments.

Finally, the demonstration of thoughtfulness and good faith in assisting the harassed and understaffed placement agency to fulfill its function is bound to improve future relations with the agency as well as with the Negro community in general.

## Relations with Educational Institutions

The Negro's drive for equal opportunity in business extends to all functional areas as well as all vertical levels. He does not expect to be hired for a job at a level which demands skills or knowledge he does not possess. However, he is demanding the right to be hired in functional areas which the company views as training grounds for potential management people. Dollars alone do not define the nature or the extent of the Negro's ambitions.

If they are ever to realize this ambition, Negroes must be persuaded to complete their schooling. College training is extremely desirable; a high school diploma is absolutely essential. The high school drop-out rate during recent years has been a major factor in producing the shortage of qualified Negroes today. The Negro's higher drop-out rate can be attributed in large part to the historical fact that possession of a high school diploma has not resulted in the same increment in lifetime earnings for Negroes as it has for whites. The average lifetime earnings differential for whites with a high school diploma vs. those without is in the neighborhood of $75,000. The differential is almost negligible for Negroes. A more vivid illustration of this same point comes from the President's Manpower Report, which states that until very recently a Negro with a college degree could expect to earn less in a lifetime than a white man with an 8th grade education.

Personnel people can do several things to combat the drop-out problem. They can approach school officials with requests to make presentations to the student body, or to interested groups of students, describing the opportunities now available in their company or in business in general for people with at least a high school education. The fact that a representative of the business community is making the initial effort to establish such a contact is bound to make a favorable impression, just because it is such an unusual occurrence. Negro as well as white speakers should be used for these presentations, in order to provide a certain "visible truth" to the remarks. Bringing in a new Negro employee especially to fill this role should be avoided in most cases, however. A question by one of the students regarding the speaker's length of employment could easily create the impression that the company was insincere and interested in public relations rather than progress.

Several companies have found it helpful to talk personally with guidance counselors of public schools and local colleges. Merely informing the guidance people of the opportunities available at his company can benefit a recruiter in terms of applicant flow. But there are additional, longer-range benefits to be gained as well.

First, the guidance counselor of a predominantly Negro school may not have much contact with business. As a result, he may know very little about the functions of business and how they relate to the high school curriculum. A business recruiter can arrange to meet with him and give him a brief description of the factors which are important for successful employment in business. According to one source, "frequently faculty members, guidance counselors, and placement officers are invited to visit employers."* With a more favorable attitude toward the business community and a better knowledge of the educational requirements which will be increasingly important in the future, a high school guidance counselor will be better able to provide inspiration and direction to students.

Second, the personnel departments can work with school administra-

---

*Robert Calvert, Jr., How to Recruit Minority Group College Graduates, p. 16.

50

tors to improve and strengthen various aspects of the total curriculum available to students. By no means are we advocating that business attempt to control curriculum development. However, to the extent that a cooperative approach by business and school personnel can be made to result in a more precise and functional definition of the educational needs of young people in today's world, students, educators and businessmen alike would benefit.

## Company Needs and Recruiting Objectives

In recruiting employees, it is usually a good practice to make sure the applicants are aware of the skill or experience qualifications of the job. In recruiting minority groups, this is especially important in order to avoid the bad inferences which may result from an "inexplicable" rejection. In order to avoid discouraging potentially good people from applying, however, several companies have developed training programs for aspiring employees who, at time of application, cannot meet the minimum standards for a particular job.

One large company has a chronic shortage of trained secretaries who are capable of taking dictation and meeting a rather demanding typing requirement. Rather than spending needless money to recruit such people from distant areas, the company has found it cheaper and more effective to set up a "school" right in its own building. The school teaches courses in stenography and typing to any employee who wishes to enroll, regardless of race, creed or color. Girls who pass a less demanding examination are hired initially into the typing pool. They take the course on company time but at no pay. When they can pass the requirements for secretary, their pay and job status are upgraded accordingly.

The effect of this program on recruiting has been twofold. First, the company has saved the expense of going outside the local community to search for people and then paying them to relocate. Second, it has become known throughout the community as a firm which takes a real interest in the growth of its people. As a result, the number of applicants and employee morale have both improved.

An example of a similar program devised specifically to meet a short-term need can be found in the recent experience of another company. This firm, a manufacturer of complex machinery, maintains a large force of engineers to provide full-line service to customers. During a recent period of a few years, qualified engineers were in short supply. To solve the problem, the company hired less qualified people, some of them Negroes, who could be rapidly trained to service the simpler lines of equipment. Then the firm temporarily revised its assignment of accounts, to allow the full-line engineers to work exclusively on the complex equipment. This required some overlapping of customer contact, but service quality was maintained. Now most of the men recruited during this period have picked up enough product knowledge to become full-line servicemen, and the overlapping contact has been eliminated.

In a third situation, a group of several companies has banded together to solve a common problem caused, as in the first illustration, by an inadequate supply of women with secretarial qualifications. The participating firms contribute the funds necessary to support a continuing thirteen-week program in typing, stenography, good grooming, etc. Enrollment is voluntary, but all applicants to the member companies who fail to meet minimum hiring standards are encouraged to attend. The only obligation for either party is that upon successful completion of the course, the students will grant interviews to the participating companies before outside organizations. Although this is the extent of the obligation, the business firms involved have experienced an understandable amount of gratitude as measured by the desire of graduates to accept offers of employment with them.

All these companies were stimulated by necessity to take such action. But, by carefully analyzing the recruiting alternatives open to them, they were able to adopt a somewhat new, untried procedure instead of the more obvious one of expanding their recruiting area. By doing so, they proved that it is possible, without jeopardizing the business, to hire and/or train people who do not initially meet minimum standards. The lesson is an important one, since it tends to expand the number of alternatives open to the recruiter.

52

## *Personal Contacts with the Negro Community*

The importance of an active effort to include the Negro in the firm's recruiting program has already been discussed. As a means of self-education regarding the Negro's environment and way of life, there is much to be said for direct personal exposure. This can be accomplished in many ways and in varying degrees.

Many whites seldom travel to or through the Negro community. A few never have. Of those who have, a great number have never taken full advantage of the opportunity to observe and reflect on some of the differences between the Negro environment and theirs. But the recruiter can hardly be effective in obtaining and hiring Negroes unless he has some basic understanding of them.

One recruiter we interviewed works for a very large national corporation. This recruiter has responsibility for filling the manpower requirements of branches in a sizable geographic area which includes both northern and southern states. He has found it does not pay to rely on his impressions of the Negro's local employment acceptance when considering applicants for a position in some distant community. Instead, he regularly makes short, routine visits to each area in his territory in order to maintain a first-hand feel for the situation in that area. By doing so he feels he can better evaluate the suitability of the applicants he has, and better prepare them to meet the challenges of their new environment once hired.

Reference was made in Chapter 3 to another personnel man in an eastern city who separated himself from his family for three months and moved to a small apartment in the Negro section of the city. Undoubtedly there are few people who would be willing to go to this extreme, and it is not our intention to imply that this is necessary. The experience is cited only to illustrate the range of commitment which is possible in this rather crucial area.

Many other opportunities exist for the effective use of direct personal contact. The recruiter should attempt to utilize the contacts and services of Negro congressmen and other community leaders. Negroes presently employed by the company should be personally appealed to for suggestions and for help in stimulating interest within the Negro community. Personnel people can take a more active role in Career Day programs in public schools and universities. They can participate on television or radio panels or public forums which discuss various aspects of the total integration problem.

*Defining the Negro Labor Supply*

The definition of the supply of recruitable Negroes should not be limited to unemployed and school-age people. There are at least two additional major resources to be investigated: Negroes employed by other business firms; Negroes employed in non-business pursuits involving transferable skills.

The former category has provided personnel for a number of companies. One firm needed a man to fill the opening created by the retirement of the business manager of the company cafeteria. The replacement had to have experience in the types of problems involved in providing food economically for large numbers of people, according to restrictive time schedules. The man finally selected—a Negro— had been the operating agent for a local catering service which the company employed for many of its major functions.

A second instance involved a company which developed an opening for an executive secretary. A Negro girl who had been in the department just a few weeks as a temporary replacement for a vacationing secretary—the Negro was employed by an outside agency which supplied temporary office help—applied for the position. She was interested in getting a job which demanded fewer changes of job location. Convinced of her qualifications, the firm hired her without spending a penny on recruiting.

These are not the only examples of this type of recruiting which could be mentioned. But most of these situations follow a similar pattern, and it is precisely the pattern which is so important. The reason becomes clear when one considers the usual initial problems of acceptance of Negroes by white work groups.

For the first few days, a Negro employee is considered in impersonal terms. To each of his associates, he is the embodiment of the general racial stereotype—he is "a Negro." This persists until the members of the work group begin to perceive more specific and more meaningful characteristics: good worker; friendly; refined; intelligent; capable; congenial; or, sloppy; incompetent; introverted; cynical; rude. In a matter of a few weeks—six weeks in the longest instance described to us—the Negro becomes accepted or rejected on his own merits as an individual, and any initial tension tends to disappear.

The significance of the "pattern" referred to above should now be clear. Both the caterer's representative and the temporary secretary had already been exposed to this initial period and had survived it. In fact, the time required for them to gain the initial acceptance of their associates was probably less than normal. Experience has shown that work groups tend to grant acceptance more readily when they believe the situation is of a temporary or "stop-gap" nature. The absence of the element of "permanence" in the initial situation reduces the resistance of the individuals involved.

Thus, the observant recruiter can often take advantage of a temporary situation where individual acceptance has already been achieved by making the association permanent. Such a technique has proven to be particularly effective in making successful "pilot placements," a term which will be described in greater detail in Chapter 6.

Frequently a recruiter will be able to find a Negro engaged in some non-business activity involving transferable skills. One firm we interviewed found an economist in a Government agency in Washington, D.C. and persuaded him to accept a position in the economic planning department. Another organization was looking for a creative writer for its advertising department and found a Negro novelist who was quite willing to turn to more productive and remunerative work.

## Sources Outside the Local Community

Most of the discussion thus far has concerned local sources of applicants. At least one major market for Negroes is basically non-local in nature, however, and that is Negro colleges.* To be sure, everything that can be said about recruiting Negroes at all-Negro colleges applies equally to integrated institutions. But the Negro universities have several needs, peculiar to them, which should be considered.

First, a recruiter should make doubly sure that the school's placement files contain as complete a story of his company as possible. It is helpful if some of this descriptive material shows Negroes working in the normal daily routine of company operations. Care must be taken to avoid a great profusion of Negroes in these illustrations, however, as any obvious attempt to oversell the company in this respect will have disastrous results.

Second, to the extent that it is feasible, the company should try to contribute some financial support to Negro universities for the purpose of teacher and curriculum development and improvement of physical facilities. The endowments of Negro institutions per student are appallingly low when compared with even the less fortunate integrated universities. Until this changes, it seems unreasonable to expect any marked improvement in the quality of preparation of the graduating students.

Third, companies can begin to play a more responsible part in the process of keeping the university leaders attuned to the changing requirements of business. It is difficult enough for placement officers and professors of integrated schools to remain current in this respect. But, the task has been historically even more difficult for Negro educators because of the severely limited contact between the Negro and business communities. Several companies are becoming actively engaged in counselling placement officers and administrators of Negro universities on business subjects. According to a recently published article;

> Lockheed Georgia has gone a step further by developing summer positions for minority group college instructors to relate industrial experience to academic instruction. Employers may want to identify outstanding minority group educators, such as Professor

---

*For a comprehensive listing of Negro colleges, see Exhibit 4 of the Appendix.

Herman Branson of Howard University, and support their teaching efforts.*

The demand for today's graduates of Negro colleges far exceeds the supply. There are complaints that many Negro graduates of these institutions are only marginally qualified. The kinds of constructive activities outlined above will serve to improve both the quality and quantity aspects of this situation. Since business stands to benefit as much as anyone from such improvement, the business community will be looked to for a commensurate contribution.

## *Implementing the Recruiting Policy*

Particular care should be taken in the selection of recruiters. It is frequently helpful to utilize Negroes in this function. However, it is usually a good idea to avoid sending Negroes out in pairs where two or more recruiters are required. This has overtones of tokenism and insincerity which the Negro may find difficult to accept.

Attention should also be given to such factors as age and background in selecting recruiters for specific assignments. One Negro personnel officer pointed out the differences in the reactions of teen-age applicants and those over thirty years of age who have directly experienced personal rejection in their own lifetimes. The use of young Negroes in recruiting assignments involving older Negro applicants had produced somewhat disappointing results.

Another piece of advice which seemed to generate unanimous agreement among the business firms studied is: "By all means avoid tokenism." Recruit for job openings that become available because of the normal operations of the business, rather than for specially created "show window" positions. State the minimum requirements for the job, and, within a range of exception similar to those described earlier, adhere to those requirements. But, if a company elects to use "None Qualified" as a reason for not hiring Negroes, it had better be fully prepared to hire one if a Negro group sends around a person who obviously does meet the stated requirements for the job. A single

---

*Calvert, loc. cit.

incident which strongly implies insincerity on the company's behalf can cause unimagined difficulties in the future.

Proper control of the recruiting effort is as necessary as it is difficult to obtain. The only meaningful test of a company's recruiting policies is: Do they tend to produce an inflow of Negro employees? Adequate feedback and control can be achieved by using periodic statistical reports from operating personnel, described in Chapter 2.

One widespread complaint among large companies concerned two unfavorable tendencies in some of the more distant branches resulting from a strong home office integration policy. First, there are the companies which market their products directly to the consumer through salesmen. The branch sales manager, seeing a possible way by which he can satisfy headquarters' desire to recruit Negroes and increase his sales at the same time, hires as many Negroes as he can find to cover the Negro community. In six months, nearly all these salesmen are forced to quit because their territory will not support them. Results: no permanent increase in sales; bad will created in the local Negro community; and an increase in the problems of recruiting.

A second circumstance concerns the harassed branch manager whose pressure to meet a sales quota is so great as to cause him to recruit Negroes indiscriminately. The adverse results have already been described in some detail in Chapter 2.

It is clear that steps should be taken to minimize the frequency of such situations. A well developed, personal understanding between headquarters and branch management is recommended as the most effective means of control. We are convinced that an awareness of these basic tendencies at the outset of an integration program will go a long way toward reducing the size of the problem.

An effective recruiting program requires, in the words of the executive vice president of a large eastern corporation, "one hell of a lot of work!" This man, who for over two years has had ultimate line authority and responsibility for the implementation of the company's progressive integration policy, spoke with the authority of experience. Nonetheless, the suggestions and ideas compiled in this chapter should remove some of the pitfalls of this difficult undertaking.

# — 5

## EVALUATING THE CRITERIA FOR SELECTION

Recruiting Negro applicants is only part of the task of bringing them into an organization. They must first be screened and, if qualified, hired. Discussions with both companies and Negro leaders indicated that a simple continuation of an organization's past practices can severely limit its ability to effect integration.

In the initial screening process, the Negro may not compare favorably with his white counterpart, when judged by historical criteria. The result has been that the number and range of jobs available to Negro applicants have been rather severely restricted.

There are basically two ways in which a company can act to change this situation. It can educate its interviewers in terms of a more realistic set of expectations for Negro applicants. In addition, it can undertake a critical evaluation of its existing hiring standards to determine the extent to which these standards are relevant to the hiring process. Since the examination of both these categories involves the controversial issue of preferential treatment, this subject will be further discussed below.

## Screening

The consensus of many corporate personnel officers, that the Negro of today usually does not measure up to his white counterpart, demands some explanation. Why should he appear differently when judged by the same standards? How is the Negro applicant actually different? To answer these questions, it is necessary to look at the normal screening process, which usually includes interviews, testing, and an examination of the applicant's relevant experience and education.

## The Interview

Why does the Negro rate differently in an interview from his white counterpart? First, his appearance is different. The clothes he wears usually reflect the styles in his community, which may not necessarily coincide with the fashions to which the interviewer is accustomed. His way of speaking and vocabulary, generally reflecting the educational level of the community he lives in, further serve to distinguish him. These factors contribute to the applicant's total effect on the interviewer.

Second, the Negro frequently does not know how to prepare for an interview or how to conduct himself during one. The principal reason for this, in most cases, is that he has not received advice concerning the proper interviewing procedures for a job applicant, and is therefore unaware of what is expected of him. Company spokesmen mentioned that this lack of counsel was most noticeable when they started interviewing at Southern Negro colleges. They discovered that applicants had not read company brochures; they knew little, if anything, about the company; and they had prepared no questions to ask the interviewer. In addition, applicants would frequently enter an interview smoking or dressed in sport clothes. If it had occurred anywhere else, this type of behavior would usually have been interpreted by the interviewers as an indication of a lack of interest. But, at these colleges, the Negroes did not know how to find out about the company; they were not aware of what material was available, and they simply did not understand what was expected of them.

These differences should not disqualify an applicant. In fact, they are the sort of things that can be changed very easily. Usually, when the Negro is placed in the normal employment environment, he is as quick as white workers to adopt the accepted standards.

Because the interviewer is likely to encounter such differences, he should be prepared to adjust to them. The personal indices of character which the interviewer has previously developed may no longer be valid when applied to Negro applicants. For instance, from his interviews with white applicants, he may have formed the notion that "sport coats are an indication of a casual attitude," or "loud colors indicate irresponsibility," or "slow speech indicates slow thinking." Such generalizations do not form a suitable frame of reference for the evaluation of a Negro applicant.

Furthermore, in order to be truly effective, an interviewer must recognize any prejudices he may have. Generally, when someone is accused of prejudice, he firmly denies the accusation. But the following example illustrates the subtle pressure which prejudice can exert in an interviewing situation.

An interviewer is to select one of two applicants for a responsible position with the company. Both applicants are qualified and could probably do a satisfactory job. One of the applicants has an outstanding record of past accomplishments. The other's record is not exceptional, but he happens to be an alumnus of the interviewer's college, or a resident of his home town, or a fraternity brother. Because of these common factors, which tend to facilitate conversation, the interviewer is very likely to be prejudiced in favor of the second applicant. Only if he recognizes this prejudice can he work to overcome it and hire the best man for the company.

A similar type of prejudice, unless it is recognized, can function against a Negro applicant. The difference in background between the applicant and the interviewer may make it considerably more difficult for the two to establish a rapport. Unless the interviewer recognizes this, he is not likely to be fair to the Negro.

Thus, the interviewer must know what differences to expect when dealing with Negro applicants. He must also realize his own prejudices and be willing to set them aside if he is to effect an honest evaluation of a Negro.

## Testing

How and why does the Negro perform differently from the non-Negro on employment tests? The answers lie in the tests themselves, as well as in the relative environments.

The acceptable standards of achievement on intelligence and aptitude tests have usually been determined in any particular firm by correlating the test scores of a large number of individuals with their levels of job performance. The pragmatic result in a predominantly white company is that the standards have been based on the culture of the group of people usually referred to as the middle and upper class segment of our population. Therefore, a bias has developed in these tests which tends to discriminate against the socio-economic stratum in which the Negro is usually classified. A brief examination of representative test questions should serve to clarify this point.

The first example involves a series of four pictures, three of which contain nothing abnormal. The applicant is instructed to select the one picture which contains a defect of some kind. The fourth picture depicts a busy living room scene, and there is a crack in one of the windows in the background. The crack might be quite obvious to someone who is not used to seeing cracked windows. However, to many Negroes, a cracked window is a very common sight. Therefore, it is unlikely that these people will identify the correct picture as readily as will a white applicant.

Another example is a visual recognition type of question which shows two corresponding sets of boxes. The first set contains photographic reproductions of a series of hand tools (such as a screw driver, a hammer, and a pair of pliers); the second set suggests possible names for the tools. The applicant is requested to match the associated boxes. These tools are all commonly found in a middle income home, as they are apt to be frequently used for building and household repairs. But the same is not true in many Negro homes.

62

Inconceivable as it may seem, a significant percentage of Negroes are unfamiliar with a simple tool such as a screw driver, because their homes do not possess a set of tools. Simple repairs are made with improvised tools (e.g , a kitchen knife is often used as a screw driver). Again, the Negro's environment places him at a disadvantage.

Both of these examples may seem difficult to believe, but they were described to us by corporate personnel officers who had had numerous contacts with the Negro community. In fact, the latter example was related by a Negro personnel recruiter.

It should be apparent from the foregoing discussion that seemingly reasonable questions can be loaded with bias against the Negroes. A few of the larger companies have recognized this and have eliminated certain questions or adjusted the specific test scores for Negroes.

A second type of test used widely as a screening mechanism measures specific skills. These achievement tests evaluate such things as a secretary's ability to type, a machinist's ability to operate a lathe, or a truck driver's response to artificial situations. If administered fairly, such examinations are extremely useful in that they can give an equitable evaluation of an applicant regardless of his race. In this respect, skills tests may present less of an obstacle to the Negro.

No matter what the type of test, however, the attitude of the individual applicant can affect his test score. For this reason, the Negro is frequently at another disadvantage when he takes an employment test. Once again, reference is made to the Negroes' attitude toward business. As discussed in the last chapter, Negroes suspect that tests have often been used in the past as an excuse for disqualifying Negroes. Whether the suspicion is fully justified is irrelevant. Its mere existence is sufficient to establish an unfavorable psychological atmosphere. Consequently, when a Negro is asked to take an employment test, he perceives business as looking for an excuse to turn him down. Such a negative attitude can easily hurt his test score.

In spite of these difficulties, testing can still be a meaningful tool for evaluating applicants. The real problem occurs when companies place too much reliance on test scores. Testing, in most cases, is not an exact science, and scores should be only one of many factors used in the final evaluation of an applicant. However, to make these test scores even more meaningful for Negro applicants, all tests should be carefully screened to eliminate questions which are inherently biased against the Negro. Also, whenever possible, tests that measure skill should supplement those that attempt to measure basic intelligence and aptitude.

## Experience and Education

It is fairly clear why Negroes will differ from whites when evaluated with respect to experience and education. In terms of experience, the Negro has been unable in the past to obtain many jobs that could provide him with worthwhile experience. It has only been in recent years that a few meaningful jobs have become available to him. For this reason, trying to hire a Negro with ten years of supervisory experience is somewhat like trying to hire an engineer with ten years of maser experience: neither is available. But in the case of the maser engineer, at least, personnel people are aware of the fact.

A similar situation exists with respect to education. With the exception of the under-utilized, well-trained Negroes, the educational background of Negro applicants is usually below that of the white applicants. The lack of a Negro "success image" in business is much to blame. It has frequently discouraged Negroes from continuing their education. This pitfall can be avoided by a careful re-examination of present job demands in relation to the qualifications required of applicants.

Frequently, when re-evaluating necessary skills for a given position, companies found that requirements and relevancy of the demands were obsolete. Many positions had acquired their characteristics through employees. Other requirements were found to be outdated by virtue of organizational, technological, or personnel changes.

The significance of this condition, for purposes of our discussion, is that companies which have analyzed their requirements have found additional jobs, now held by whites, that are also suitable for Negroes, given their current experience and education levels. Frequently, these jobs could offer a Negro sufficient experience to allow him to progress eventually to positions of significant responsibility. Far too few of these training positions are available for Negroes today.

As was mentioned in Chapter 1, there is little pressure today to place Negroes in significant management positions. However, this situation is most probably not going to continue indefinitely. By starting Negroes up the proper advancement ladders today, companies can avoid the pressure to do so in the future. Furthermore, they will have qualified Negroes on their management teams. Since these are the terms in which companies should be planning today, a thorough analysis of job requirements would seem to be a necessary step for effective integration.

## *Analysis of Job Requirements*

Such an analysis should start with an examination of the job and the qualifications of the person holding it. What type of work is involved? How much of the required training can be given on the job? What background is necessary for the employee to absorb this training? Where is a man likely to progress from this position? Does this next step have any prerequisites that need to be included in the entry requirements for the initial job? Answers to questions such as these will facilitate the development of meaningful requirements.

While answers are being developed, thought should be given to determining what tests, if any, should be used for screening, and what previous experience or education should be required. By going through this process, with the knowledge of how the Negro applicant will differ from the white applicant, management of a company can eliminate a great deal of the bias which has existed in the past. In addition, by considering on-the-job training, the new requirements will place even more positions within the reach of Negro applicants.

A critical examination of various positions often reveals that some, realistically, should have two sets of requirements. Usually, these are positions where it is desirable to allow rapid promotion for a few, while maintaining a suitable base of long-service employees. In this category, it is best to hire some people with the intention of promoting them, while hiring others into initial jobs on a more permanent basis. Two sets of requirements are therefore appropriate.

An example of a situation where a dual job classification is suitable may make this more explicit. A national concern that sells directly to the home through route salesmen hired a consulting concern to determine what kind of men it should be hiring.* The research started with a study of the existing sales force. It was found that the present salesmen tended to fit into one of three distinct categories based on: 1) the way they organized and handled their work; 2) their ability to cope with the demands of the company; 3) their own needs and expectations. The groups included the stable, satisfied men; the ambitious men; and the disorganized or unstable men.

The stable man derived his greatest satisfaction from his comfortable, friendly relationship with his customers. He saw his job as a permanent thing and easily coped with pressures placed on him by the company. He was seen as the ideal routeman.

The ambitious routeman regarded his job as a step toward a higher position. He was more detached and had less basic need for long, pleasant, friendly interpersonal relationships with his customers. Therefore, he more easily accepted the work of a supervisor, which involved a large number of relatively impersonal and brief contacts with people. His satisfaction came from accomplishment of tasks rather than from friendly relationships. This man was an ideal prospect for advancement in the company. In fact, without rapid advancement, he was likely to leave.

The disorganized or unstable routeman was generally unable to cope with his work and therefore made a very poor routeman.

The recommendation of the consulting firm was that: 1) unstable, disorganized men should be avoided; 2) ambitious men should be hired within the limits set by anticipated supervisory openings; 3) stable,

---

*J. Sterling Livingston and Robert T. Davis, Cases in Sales Management, p. 28.

well-organized men should be hired to fill the majority of positions that became available.

Although this study is not specifically related to Negroes, it does illustrate how two very different types of individuals can effectively be used for the same position. It would seem possible to apply this same reasoning to many different jobs. The objective behind establishing what is essentially a high and a low standard for certain jobs is not to offer preference to Negroes, but to open up new positions where they can realistically compete with white applicants.

As long as a supervisor is willing to promote on the basis of ability once the men are hired, such a system can operate satisfactorily. The men in a work group can understand why a peer is promoted. On the other hand, if the supervisor becomes lazy and promotes only those men who were preselected to be promoted, without considering their performance in relation to men in the "permanent" pool, morale can suffer. Supervisors should therefore be cautioned against doing this since passing up a "permanent" Negro who is suitable for promotion could lead to charges of discrimination. Because this dual requirement system is dependent on the supervisor's ability to judge promotability, rather than on seniority, it is not suitable in instances where "seniority rules" are too confining, as is often the case with many union jobs.

If a working relationship has been established with Negro leaders, it may be worthwhile for the company to explain to them the strategy behind these dual requirement jobs. Once such a plan is understood, it will be appreciated rather than misinterpreted as discrimination.

## Preferential Treatment

Chapter 1 posed the question, "What is business' responsibility with respect to integration?" Indeed, it would be difficult to find agreement on one answer to that question. However, our study indicated mutual agreement on the opinion that business must share a portion of the responsibility for the present economic level of the Negro community.

Given this admission, there was still a broad spectrum of feelings as to exactly what business' future obligations should be. At one end of the spectrum is the company whose executives are reluctant to admit that there has been any bias in the past with respect to hiring. They feel that the full extent of the company's responsibility consists of offering "equal opportunity" to any Negroes who voluntarily seek employment. With this attitude, they will accomplish little.

Next is the company whose management admits that although they have not been biased, they have not been attracting Negro applicants. They are usually willing to start a recruiting program to attract Negroes and will hire them on the basis of the firm's present selection criteria. If they have two applicants for one position, they will hire the most qualified, even if the other was an adequately qualified Negro. Given two equally qualified applicants, the bias built into existing selection criteria would most likely cause them to hire the white applicant rather than the Negro.

Management of one such company defended hiring the most qualified person by saying that they were not hiring a man for any one position, but for a career with the company. They hoped to be able to promote all new employees within the year of their hiring. Therefore, they argued that the idea of using minimal requirements was not suitable for their organization.

Next on the spectrum is the company frankly admitting that, although no bias was intended, it has existed. To correct the situation, it is willing to adopt an active recruiting program for Negroes. Further, it is willing to make an analysis of its employment requirements in order to put the maximum number of employment opportunities within reach of Negro applicants. Given two qualified applicants, one white and one Negro, this firm might offer the job to the Negro.

The experience of a large manufacturing company provides an excellent example of this type of preference. This company had a yearly "skilled crafts" training program which was traditionally filled by graduates from local high schools. Since there were always a great number (over 120) of applicants, members of top management had established an elaborate system for ranking them  In 1963, they wanted 35 people for the training program. According to the ranking procedure, the first 42 positions were held by white applicants, while Negroes occupied the 43rd and 45th places. After careful consideration of the pertinent entry requirements, management decided that any of the top 50 individuals would be suitable. In order to give the two Negroes an opportunity, the company hired the first 33 people and then completed the program with numbers 43 and 45. As a point of interest, the two Negroes have performed better than a number of their white associates.

At the most liberal extreme are companies willing to make selective compromises in their standard criteria to accommodate the Negro's situation. These companies are making a sincere and concerted effort to help the Negro whenever they feel it is possible.

A good example involves a food manufacturer who had hired a Negro salesman to call on supermarket accounts. The company's personnel people had hired this man even though he lacked a driver's license, a major qualification for the job. He was hired on the understanding that within a certain period of time he was to get the license. The Negro obtained his learner's permit and was able to learn how to drive during the first few days while his supervisor was traveling his route with him. The willingness on the part of the company to adapt its policy to match an individual situation allowed the company to offer employment to this otherwise well-qualified Negro.

A large consumer goods company with plants throughout the United States provides an even stronger illustration of what some firms are willing to do. The president of this organization, while visiting one location, asked the plant manager about the progress of his integration effort. The plant manager replied that he had been quite successful, but with one exception—he had been unable to locate any qualified Negro machinists. The president replied by asking the plant manager what he would have done to obtain qualified machinists during World War II when only 4F's were available. The manager answered: "Train them, I suppose," to which the president simply gave an affirmative nod. His point had been adequately made. It was estimated by the manager who was recounting this instance that probably within hours every plant manager knew of this episode.

A third example, and one very similar to the preceding one, is provided by a large state-wide service organization. Executives of this firm have been trying to establish an arrangement with a local college to provide night school classes for both Negro and white applicants who cannot meet the minimum education requirements. These executives realize that if such a program could be developed, it would allow them to bring many more qualified Negroes into their organization sooner.

All these examples demonstrate some of the methods businesses have used to make significant contributions to the task of elevating the economic and educational level of the Negro community to that of the national average. These companies have been able to make their contributions because they were willing to assume the small additional risk of hiring Negroes and part of the responsibility for training them. It would be folly to deny that this is, in a sense, preferential treatment. Nevertheless, these are the types of actions that business can and must take to make integration an eventual reality.

It seems clear that business, by changing some of its hiring practices, can make a significant contribution to a problem that is currently facing the entire country. It is the job of each individual firm to determine how much it needs to change and what its responsibility is. Government and Negro group pressures certainly cannot be ignored in this determination process, and, to some extent, they may dictate the minimum changes to be made.

The majority of the work outlined in this chapter will naturally become the responsibility of the personnel office. However, it should be remembered that the final decision as to whether an applicant is hired often is made by operating people. The bias which these individuals can introduce should not be ignored. In fact, the personnel office should make a concerted effort to devise some method of dealing with this bias. This suggests the desirability of careful investigation when a Negro applicant, considered well qualified by the personnel office, has been rejected by an operating manager.

# — 6

## CREATING AND MAINTAINING
## A CONSTRUCTIVE ENVIRONMENT

Having hired a Negro, the company then faces the challenge of where to place and how to use the Negro, and how to facilitate his acceptance by the other employees. Unlike contacting, recruiting, and hiring Negroes, this challenge is basically an internal one, although there may be some surveillance of the company's actions by various interested outside parties. While the external functions of contacting, recruiting, and hiring directly concern a very small percentage of the company's work force, absorption of the Negro directly affects the entire corporate populace. Implementing the first three functions necessitates "kid-glove" tactics with regard to the Negro leaders and applicants. Although many of these tactics must be continued to some degree after the Negro is hired, the handling of the in-house work force requires finesse of a different kind.

### Work Force Preparation

The consensus of the personnel men interviewed in this study was that company personnel should be informed of the steps being taken toward Negro integration. There was also fairly general agreement that the specific work groups into which the first Negroes were being hired should be prepared for their arrival. But there was a vast divergence of opinion as to the extent to which the work force should be kept informed of integration proceedings and the amount of preparation to be given the specific work group. Each opinion was supported by many individual experiences. The following case demonstrates an approach which appeared to be very satisfactory.

A large industrial company with approximately fifteen percent of its facilities in the South decided to integrate a certain Mid-South plant. It chose, as a first step, to bring a Negro girl into a secretarial pool for an engineering group. Each girl in the pool was taken aside and individually informed that a Negro was being hired to work in her group. Depending on her reaction, one of a number of approaches was taken. For the most part, the girls were simply assured that the newcomer was just as qualified a secretary as they. The girls were asked individually what they wanted from their jobs. Then, each girl was told as logically as possible that the incoming Negro girl wanted essentially the same things.

Following these private conferences, the entire group was assembled. The girls were told that this undertaking was a test of the "American way," and that further efforts along this line would be affected by the results exhibited by their group. Then the personnel manager asked if there were any objections. The two girls who objected were counseled again regarding the reasons why integration was taking place in their plant. In these counseling sessions, it was also implied that they would not be allowed to change jobs within the company.

A few days later, after some personal preparation, the Negro girl was brought in. Some of the girls, including one of the objectors, had lunch with her the first day. It took only a short while for the Negro girl to demonstrate her abilities, and within three weeks she was accepted as one of the group. But the most interesting part of this story is that just before the Negro was brought in, the entire pool sought out the personnel manager and said that the company had waited much too long to start integrating, that Negroes deserved a decent break, and that they were honored to have been selected as the group for the initial experiment! To quote: "We think you picked us because you thought we were more flexible and better Americans than the girls in Accounting."

The preceding case illustrates three essential steps in absorbing the first Negroes into a group. First, it is extremely helpful to have the personnel officer and the department manager conduct individual conferences with the department employees. This is one of the best ways to find out which employees are going to be disturbed by the action and which ones the company can depend on for help. Obviously, a department manager has some prior idea of the attitudes of his subordinates, but in these conferences managers can begin to anticipate and correct potential problems on an individual basis.

Second, assembling the entire group is very important in developing group acceptance, since it tends to mold the initial group sentiment along positive lines. One criterion for the selection of the initial group should be the presence of informal group leaders who can be counted on for support of integration efforts. Even the most recalcitrant employee can be won over by group persuasion and a Negro who is capable and personable.

Third, management should try to secure an immediate demonstration of a reasonable attitude by the group. This is not always forthcoming as it was in the above example, but in a pilot placement it is highly desirable for its effect both on the Negro and on the rest of the plant or company.

It should be apparent that in the initial placement, the selection of the group to be integrated is at least as important as the selection of the specific Negro to be employed. This point also applies to the prior preparation of the group to be integrated. A final point contained in the above illustration, and one deserving strong emphasis, is that the problem of absorbing the newly hired Negro into the existing environment is vastly over-rated. It is, to quote the Executive Vice-President of a major industrial firm, "...just like any other operating problem."

## Selection of the Initially Hired Negroes

Because the initial implementation is so essential to further success, the Negro obviously must be selected with great care, and the preparation program must be developed to suit the individual case. Since the Urban League has participated in many pilot placements, it can often be of invaluable assistance in the selection and preparation of the first Negro employee. The League will pre-screen and forward applicants to a company and will make a considerable effort to select and prepare the applicants for their interviews and possible employment.

In discussing the requisite qualifications of the first Negro, there was found to be an apparent conflict of opinion between companies and the League. Most companies felt that the initial Negroes should be over-qualified, while the League argued strongly that a company should place the Negro in a job which was commensurate with his abilities. As the interviews proceeded, however, it became clear that there was actually no conflict at all. The companies prefer to seek Negroes who are above average in their ability to get along with people, and whose personalities will enable them to weather any initial discrimination within the work group. Very few firms actually demand that the Negro be technically over-qualified. The League is convinced that the technical qualifications required of a pilot placement are no greater than those necessitated by the work. However, in its pre-screening, the League looks for people whose personalities will allow them to gain rapid acceptance, and who are capable of proving their competence fairly quickly.

Both parties agree, then, that the pilot placement must be over-qualified from the standpoint of social maturity and tolerance. It is not necessary, however, for an initial placement to possess technical qualifications greater than those required by the job in which he is placed. The practice of demanding technical over-qualifications can be a real danger for two reasons. First, the Negro will quickly become dissatisfied with an unchallenging job, and the possibility of losing him will be high, due to the present market demand for skilled Negroes. If the Negro

74

elects to accept a more attractive offer from another company, a great deal of recruiting and preparatory effort will have been wasted.

Second, it will be harder for the members of the work group to accept a Negro who accomplishes a great deal more than they do. Very quickly a barrier will be erected between a "norm-breaking Negro" and the majority of the group. On the other hand, a Negro whose efforts and productivity are more in line with those of his white fellows will be accepted and respected readily as a hard-working associate.

## Preparation of the Initially Hired Negroes

If the hired Negro fully satisfies the above requirements, a minimal amount of preparation will be required in addition to the normal indoctrination process. It should be necessary only for the department manager and the personnel officer to have one or two meetings with him to demonstrate their sincerity and interest in keeping things running smoothly. It will not be at all difficult for the Negro to realize the problems he could create for himself and future Negro employees by not accepting most of the responsibility for developing a workable relationship within the group. Nearly every personnel manager contacted, who had participated in a pilot placement, acknowledged the responsibility demonstrated by Negroes carefully selected for such placement. Quite obviously, some cases will require more counseling than others. Generally, though, a great deal of counseling is not necessary with pilot placements because of the type of person sought. As the number of Negro hirings increases, the ability to find persons qualified on a personality basis will decline, and more counseling may be required. Conversely, less preparation of the work force will be necessary.

## Preparation of Subsequently Hired Negroes

Earlier chapters discussed policies concerning technical training prior to and following placement of a Negro. Basically, this kind of training entails only the upgrading of skills and is a problem of locating the necessary teachers and funds.

The actual integration of these new employees requires some social and personal preparation. Both Negro leaders and personnel managers indicated that the average Negro is, in many cases, somewhat ill-prepared psychologically and socially. However, through pre-job counseling, particularly by his future supervisor and by the Negro leaders working with a company, the Negro can quickly overcome this difficulty. Many Negroes are understandably frightened by a new job. They are often sensitive to criticism by a white supervisor. The supervisor can alleviate this initial tension by praising the Negro when he does well, and by criticizing his mistakes in a constructive manner, free from condescending overtones.

Because supervisory personnel are so crucial to the success of the absorption process, their actions should be controlled by an effective reporting system, details of which were described in Chapter 2. As a further means of insuring a supervisor's good faith and active participation, several personnel officers recommended that top management utilize the "economic stick," making it clear that a supervisor risks losing his job if his actions fail to support corporate policies.

As one very important corporate policy, a company's integration program should be regularly included as a discussion topic at top level meetings. This will insure a continuing awareness on the part of all departments of the importance placed on it by company executives. It will also prevent good initial efforts from tapering off.

## Desegregation of Facilities

In conjunction with changes in attitudes related to hiring, a company should also undertake to eliminate segregation from its facilities and functions. This problem is not confined to the South. Personnel officers of many Northern-based companies have described various desegregation measures they have undertaken. These measures pertain to tacit agreements between company and union as to the opportunity for Negro advancement. Some personnel men also spoke of the elimination of such practices as giving a Negro ten dollars to take his wife to dinner on the night of a company party to be held at a "segregated" hotel.

The hypocrisy of a management which condones the practices of segregation, while ostensibly supporting a program of equal employment, will be obvious both within and without the organization. The outcome will be a rapid deterioration of the hiring program.

The problem of desegregating facilities is obviously somewhat greater in the South than in the North, particularly as regards the elimination of segregated social functions. But the successful resolutions of such problems, as related to us by several personnel managers who had recently integrated facilities in their Southern plants, entails only the application of a policy of firmness and patience.

For example, a large industrial company with several Southern plants decided to desegregate its shower rooms. This involved the unlocking of a door between the "Colored" shower room and the unmarked shower room adjacent to it. On the first day, three Negroes asked for lockers on the formerly white side. The local personnel manager, Mr. Smith, called the corporate personnel director, Mr. Jones, and asked what he should do. He was promptly instructed to give the Negroes the lockers which they had requested. The next day Mr. Smith called again to say that about six Negroes had used the white showers, and about ten whites had gone home without showering. Mr. Jones merely replied, "Well, I guess we've got six clean colored boys and ten dirty white ones today." Within a week the showers were fully integrated and no one was going home without showering. On two occasions during the first week, someone repainted "Colored" on one shower room, and both times the company painted over it without a word. Firm but patient enforcement accomplished, without incident, a desegregation that many thought would take months and entail serious difficulties. The company began by integrating a facility which everyone either had to use or be willing to endure a certain amount of physical discomfort. Progress from then on was undisturbed. Of course, all desegregation moves are not so easy, but the large majority of the people we interviewed had encountered no serious problems when they displayed firmness in the face of pressure applied by diehards within their work forces.

## Problems Regarding the Firing of Negroes

The problem of firing a Negro recently hired into a position which no Negro has previously held is more disturbing than a normal release, in that extra time and money were expended in recruiting the Negro. There is also the fear of accusations of discrimination both from the former Negro employee and from the local Negro leaders. To minimize the bad effects of such a necessity, a procedure should be established to insure that bias is not the reason for Negro releases. Obviously the best way to obtain this insurance would be to place the Negro at the very outset in a position under the least biased supervisor, but this is not always possible and does not always eliminate the problem. Another method is for the personnel manager to assure himself, by investigating individual situations, that the reason for the firing is not simple bias on the supervisor's part or discriminatory practices within the Negro's work group. If the man deserves to be fired, maintenance of employee morale and corporate integrity demands that he be fired. If he was merely reacting to discrimination by other employees, it might be best to transfer him to another group and avoid possible external reactions.

Before releasing a Negro, the company should consult with the Negro leaders with whom it is in contact. Virtually all of the Negro leaders interviewed said that a company's retention of a Negro who should be fired harmed relations between the company and the Negro community. They felt such a man should be fired before more harm occurred. A Negro who fails to do his job and is disruptive causes bias to form within his work group and company, and this is precisely what the Negro leaders are opposing. Therefore, if they are informed of the reasons for a Negro's release, they will usually work to minimize any possible after-effects.

In situations where a company desires the advice of Negro leaders regarding the best way of effecting the dismissal, it will usually find such advice to be constructive. Negro leaders can also be of assistance in determining the cause of the firing, as they will obviously be searching for signs of discrimination. The discovery of discrimination would be valuable to the company in two respects: 1) it would prevent the unwarranted discharge of an expensively recruited employee; 2) it would pinpoint a potential problem area and help correct the cause of the discrimination.

In some cases, the Negro leaders may be forced to protest the firing regardless of the situation, just as a union is often obliged to support the grievances of its members. However, if the Negro leaders are made fully aware of the reasons for the discharge, their protests will take the form of minimal political gestures rather than vigorous action.

## Programs for Advancement of Negroes

Providing the opportunity to upgrade personal skills equally with the rest of the work force must be an integral part of any successful integration program. Actions which can be taken to insure equal opportunity in this regard include the removal of any discriminatory clauses from the labor contract and the establishment of training programs covering the basic requirements for advancement to higher level positions. The following case provides a good illustration of a successful upgrading program.

At a mid-Southern plant of a large industrial company, a considerable amount of automation was taking place, and many new skills were being required of the labor force. The company gave a series of tests to determine which employees could handle the newly created jobs. A number of employees failed to pass the tests, and it appeared that they would have to be eliminated from the work force. Nearly all of these employees were Negroes. The company decided to conduct a voluntary school after working hours on company property and free of charge for any employee who had not passed the test. Elementary and advanced classes were conducted in reading, writing and arithmetic of the nature that would be required in the future.

To date, nearly 180 employees have completed the school and have been placed in jobs handling the automated machinery. The total cost to the company has been very low. In many cases, this type of special treatment is necessary to provide an opportunity for the Negro laborer to advance. Such services certainly need not be restricted to Negro employees. But, as a group, they can normally be expected to benefit more from such programs, because a higher percentage of them need the extra training.

## Promotion to Supervisory Positions

Discrimination exists in the process of promotion to supervisory levels basically because of management's fear that white subordinates will rebel against a Negro supervisor. However, in most cases where Negroes have been appointed supervisors, this fear of white resistance has not been realized. In fact, the most frequent source of problems has been the desire of Negro members of the work group to see whether the new supervisor will give his fellow Negroes preferential treatment. Generally, this period of trial is brief. If the company has promoted the right man, it will rapidly become evident to all concerned that no one gets a better deal because of his skin color.

The experience of several companies indicated very little white resistance to the promotion of a Negro, when the Negro had gained acceptance as an equal prior to the promotion. As one manager expressed it, "Promote the man who is actually the informal group leader, no matter what color he is, and everything will be all right." A "color-blind" promotion policy, backed by simple but firm implementation, is normally quite effective. Companies utilizing this approach have found that the promotion of Negroes to supervisory positions is no more a problem than the initial absorption of Negroes into the work force.

# — 7

# CASE STUDIES

The following two case studies of contrasting reactions of management to pressures for racial integration illustrate the composite impact of the numerous issues and suggestions discussed in preceding chapters. The first case describes events culminating in the boycott of a bank; the second presents the integration efforts of a consumer goods company. Names, places, and dates have been disguised to preserve the anonymity of information obtained in confidence.

## The Second National Bank

The Second National Bank is a medium-sized institution with 25 branches in a large Eastern city with a Negro concentration of 10%. Although Negroes account for 15% of its business, the Second National, like most banks in the area, has for a long time been lax about integrating its work force. Of its 620 employees, in the spring of 1963, six were Negroes, and they were all janitors.

The bank's president, Mr. McDevit, had been a leader in local community affairs for many years and assisted in sponsoring the "Negro Savings Bank" immediately after World War II. He was somewhat surprised, therefore, in March of 1963, when he received a letter from Mr. Thompson, head of a local Negro organization, accusing his bank of discrimination. After some delay, Mr. McDevit responded, stating that he was personally unaware of any prejudice in his bank, but suggesting a meeting between Mr. Thompson and his personnel director, Mr. Weld, to discuss the matter. During the next two months, Mr. Thompson and Mr. Weld met unproductively several times. Mr. Weld continued to insist that the bank had been a merit employer in the past. Although he admitted that there were very few Negroes on the payroll, he countered that this was the case because no qualified Negroes had ever applied. Furthermore, Mr. Weld cited the bank's large volume of loans to Negroes in support of his contention that the bank had also been nondiscriminatory in its allocation of funds.

Mr. Thompson, however, was not satisfied, and he felt that the fact that less than 1% of the bank's employees were Negroes was sufficient proof of discriminatory practices. In support of his conviction, he showed Mr. Weld the application form of a Negro who had applied for a job as teller and had been turned down. The Negro's qualifications were nearly identical to those of a white CORE tester who had been accepted. Although Mr. Weld agreed that the incident had been an unfortunate one, he claimed it had been done only because the bank's officers were of the opinion that the customers of the particular branch involved were not yet ready to accept a Negro teller. Mr. Thompson did not consider this reasoning convincing, nor were his doubts dispelled when, shortly thereafter, the Second National hired its seventh Negro employee as a teller and Mr. McDevit became an active member of the local Urban League.

In September 1963, Mr. Thompson sent letters to each member of the Second National's board of directors urging the board to adopt a policy of merit employment. All letters were promptly answered, with each director expressing his concern and promising to look into the matter at the October board meeting. Mr. Thompson had no further communication with the bank until he wrote a letter to Mr. McDevit requesting information concerning the outcome of the board meeting. The reply, which came from the personnel manager, stated that the directors had concluded that the bank had been pursuing an equal opportunity policy in the past and would continue to do so in the future.

Should any qualified Negroes apply for loans or for job openings when they became available, they would be given equal consideration with white applicants. If Mr. Thompson had any specific cases of discrimination which he wished to pursue, the bank would be happy to discuss such matters with him.

Mr. Thompson regarded the letter as unacceptable and decided to boycott the bank. Early in March, he organized demonstrators for a boycott to take place on a Wednesday. On the Tuesday afternoon preceding the day of the boycott, police notified Mr. McDevit regarding the proceedings scheduled for Wednesday. Mr. McDevit quickly arranged a meeting with Mr. Thompson for 7:00 a.m. the next morning in order to try to avoid the boycott. This meeting constituted the first face-to-face encounter between Mr. McDevit and Mr. Thompson. Despite a rather heated discussion, Mr. McDevit persuaded Mr. Thompson to give the bank a week to try to meet the Negro demands.

The only critical area of disagreement during the negotiations had been over the Negroes' demands to be informed of the salaries and descriptions of each position in the bank. Mr. Thompson felt that the possession of this information would help his people to formulate more realistic demands as to how soon and how many Negroes the bank should employ. Mr. McDevit agreed to consider the matter during an emergency board of directors meeting and to inform Mr. Thompson of the result within a week. On the following Monday, he presented the Negroes with a list of bank positions. The list did not include the positions of janitors or officers of the bank, and no reference was made to salaries. When Mr. Thompson reiterated his request for salary information, Mr. McDevit asserted that this data was confidential and could not be released, even though the Negroes promised to keep it in confidence.

Negotiations ceased, and the next day a boycott began. It lasted for two weeks. During the first week, Mr. McDevit managed to keep the boycott out of the papers and his only difficulty was with the fifteen of twenty demonstrators who picketed in front of the entrance to his main office. By the end of the first week, Mr. Thompson felt that his demonstrators were not receiving enough publicity, and he directed them to become more belligerent in their picketing. Only with the help of police were customers able to enter the bank during the second week.

The wide publicity given by the press to the incidents of those last several days included a challenge by the Negroes to debate publicly the matter with members of the bank. The bank's response was a refusal even to consider the possibility of public debates, and a continuation of the request for police assistance in restraining the demonstrators—who Mr. McDevit described as the "dregs of society."

Although the publicity of the demonstrations was having little immediate effect on business, management felt that the reputation of the Second National was suffering, and at the end of the second week the Negroes were persuaded to stop the demonstrations and resume negotiations. In an attempt to reduce the tension which had developed between Mr. McDevit and Mr. Thompson, the bank hired an outside mediator to handle the negotiations. The move was not helpful, however, as the Negroes interpreted it as a sign that management would not condescend to deal with Negroes directly. Finally, Mr. McDevit returned to the negotiations himself. After considerable discussion, a temporary settlement was reached whereby the bank agreed to attempt actively to hire additional Negroes.

In retrospect, it seems fairly clear that this boycott could have been avoided. Mr. McDevit contended that the Negroes—thinking that he sympathized with their cause and would give in easily—had decided to boycott his establishment no matter what he did. But there is little evidence to support this interpretation. Other companies contacted by Mr. Thompson had avoided boycotts by pursuing relatively mild integration policies. One department store had developed such close relations with Mr. Thompson that he privately encouraged Negroes to shop at that store. This relationship was established through relatively small gestures, such as letting Mr. Thompson know each time a job opening occurred.

It is particularly significant that Mr. McDevit met Mr. Thompson for the first time at 7:00 a.m. on the morning of the scheduled boycott, certainly not the best environment for developing a sound working relationship. Had Mr. McDevit gotten to know Mr. Thompson earlier, he would have observed the man's strong pride and sincere desire to be accepted by whites. By inviting Mr. Thompson to lunch, Mr. McDevit could probably have radically altered his attitude toward the Second National Bank. Instead, Mr. McDevit constantly snubbed Mr. Thompson. Behind his back, he began supporting a rival Negro organization in an attempt to weaken Mr. Thompson's bargaining position. He also persisted in referring Mr. Thompson to the personnel director rather than handling the matter himself, and even neglected to answer Mr. Thompson's letters promptly.

It seems unlikely that Mr. McDevit would thus have risked alienating a white customer who represented 15% of the bank's loans, or whose actions could cost the bank thousands of dollars in lost business and legal fees.

## *The Maxwell Company*

Most of the businessmen we talked to in the course of the study did their best, we are confident, to be candid in their replies. However, the sensitive nature of the subject matter naturally tempts management to minimize the actual problems encountered and maximize the contribution of a particular company in its integration effort. The attempt was made to maintain a balanced viewpoint by meeting with Negro leaders in order to hear their versions of the progress of specific companies.

In one case in particular, the Negro and company descriptions of a sequence of events and their consequences were in extremely close agreement. Since this case illustrates the successful use of many of the policies suggested in this report, some of its more important aspects will be described on the following pages.

The Maxwell Company processes and markets consumer products throughout 15 middle-Atlantic and East Central States. Products are marketed both indirectly through retail outlets and directly to the consumer through home route-men.

By the latter part of 1962, management at Maxwell was becoming increasingly concerned about the deteriorating climate of race relations throughout its area of operations. Picketing of business and public institutions was becoming a more frequent occupation of the active Negro groups in the area. Selective patronage had been tried with moderate to remarkable success in recent months. In addition, the use of "bias-control" interviewing teams by CORE and NAACP was being rapidly expanded.* Several consumer goods firms in Maxwell's market area had been embarrassed by such incidents in recent months. The combined impact of these trends was sufficient to motivate Maxwell's top management to take a critical look at Maxwell's position.

As was the case with several of the firms which had already fallen prey to Negro pressures, Maxwell had had a long-standing policy of non-discriminatory hiring. Despite this fact, a "head-count" indicated that the percentage of Negroes employed in the headquarters offices was less than one-fourth of the percentage of Negro residents in the surrounding metropolitan community. Furthermore, most of these Negroes were employed in low-level, "non-visible" positions that had traditionally offered little opportunity for advancement in status or responsibility. Conversations with Negro employees and community leaders indicated that Maxwell had the reputation of being a "white employer."

An analysis of personnel records yielded some clues as to how such a situation had probably developed in the face of an obviously contradictory employment policy. First, the company's main establishment was located in a white section of town. Therefore, the

---

*This is a technique whereby white and Negro volunteers work in pairs, the pairing in any particular case being determined by the hiring requirements of the company to be contacted. A company is selected which is known to have certain job openings and which is suspected of being a discriminatory employer. The white individual selected for the interviewing team will meet all of the company's hiring standards, but will still be less qualified than his Negro counterpart. The Negro will apply first, followed by the white. If the company should hire or even give positive encouragement to the white interviewee while rejecting or adopting a noncommittal attitude toward the Negro, it will be contacted immediately by representatives of the sponsoring Negro organization and required to explain its actions.

location had tended, over time, to reduce the number of Negro applicants.

Second, in an attempt to minimize recruiting costs and maximize employees' satisfaction with their working associates, Maxwell's personnel people had actively encouraged employees to submit references of prospective applicants. Since the ratio of Negroes in the work force was very small, this procedure also acted to inhibit the number of Negro applicants.

Third, low employee turnover at nearly all levels contributed to the strong forces opposing the recruitment and hiring of non-white individuals. Regardless of how unconscious or coincidental its causes might have been, a discriminatory bias had become institutionalized in Maxwell's employment practices which would be difficult to explain to even the most understanding Negro leaders.

At about the same time that Maxwell's management personnel were arriving at these conclusions, two events occurred which precipitated the decision to take immediate action. A neighboring firm having a product and market structure similar to Maxwell's was struck by a selective patronage campaign which very quickly reduced its sales by 33 per cent. Rumors were heard from several sources that Negro leaders were considering Maxwell as their next target. Maxwell's top management promptly decided to take the initiative by voluntarily adopting a progressive program designed to insure better opportunity for Negroes at Maxwell.

Meeting together, they defined five fundamental objectives of the plan:

1. To stimulate greater effort by operating personnel in seeking qualified Negro applicants;
2. To develop agreement among operating personnel on a constructive program designed to overcome the possible objections to Negro employees in certain job classifications, whether these objections originated from customers or from other employees;
3. To avoid pressures and possible selective patronage campaigns by Negro organizations;
4. To comply more closely in actual practice with state and federal fair employment laws;
5. To assume Maxwell's share of social responsibility for improving the status of minority groups.

Having a clear working definition of the goals to be achieved, Maxwell's management next embarked on what could well be the most crucial undertaking in the establishment of a positive integration policy: the initial dissemination of descriptive material to lower levels of operating management. The successful implementation of any top management policy depends ultimately on the cooperation and support of all levels of management. The difficulty of winning that support can depend a great deal on the manner in which top executives choose to communicate their position.

Members of upper management were very successful in creating a workable, receptive atmosphere at Maxwell. Their extensive memorandum to all management personnel began with a statement of the objectives delineated above. This was followed by a summary of the integration problem in general, as well as the recent local trends and activities as they related to Maxwell. Additional background information was provided through the distribution of several recent articles from management journals.*

Having established the need for adopting a positive course of action, top management next turned to the problem of calming anxieties which might arise in managers' minds with respect to customer and employee reactions. For this purpose, data had been compiled on the number of complaints, new starts, and terminations of service on the home delivery routes. Statistics showing initial results for Negro route-men on newly assigned routes, as well as over extended periods of time, proved to be comparable in every significant respect with the results for white route-men.†  The only real problem in Maxwell's experience in this area had been caused by the hiring of two Negro route-men who were not competent to handle the basic requirements of the job, and who quit after less than a week on the job.

As an added assurance to sales managers, however, top manage-

_____

*Caroline Bird, "More Room at the Top," Management Review, 52:4-16, March, 1963; "Guidelines for Initiating Fair Employment Practices," Personnel, 53-59, May-June, 1963; and John Perry, "Business—Next Target for Integration, "Harvard Business Review, March-April, 1963.

†At this time the company employed five Negro route-men.

ment described a "sales kitty" which was to be set up to reimburse managers for any abnormal sales losses resulting from the introduction of a Negro route-man. (Management reports that after a year of the new policy, the kitty remains untapped.)

The memorandum ended with a statement declaring top management's complete and sincere commitment to the task. In accordance with Maxwell's policy of decentralized authority and responsibility, the actual implementation of the policy would be left largely in the hands of operating managers. However, regular monthly reports would be required of all levels in order to enable top management to evaluate periodically Maxwell's status relative to the percentage concentration of Negroes in the surrounding population.

In the weeks immediately following the distribution of the memorandum, managers at all levels held numerous meetings with their associates for the purpose of airing possible objections and developing satisfactory answers to them. It was hoped that this type of activity would help to weld all management personnel together in mutual support of the plan proposed by top management.

In implementing its program, Maxwell utilized many of the concepts suggested earlier in this report. Company personnel established close contacts with ministers, leaders of local branches of the various Negro organizations and school guidance counselors. Job openings were listed regularly with general and minority-group employment agencies. Agency directors were frequently contacted by telephone and encouraged to participate in solving current recruiting and placement problems.

Company representatives participated in community career conferences and as speakers at church and social center gatherings.

Articles were run in the Maxwell magazine to keep employees informed and interested in the progress of the program. Personnel people followed up these articles by meeting with present Negro employees to encourage them to submit names of Negroes they considered to be potentially qualified applicants.

Job opportunities at Maxwell were published in the local Negro newspapers as well as in the usual white dailies. Fliers were mailed to community and church social centers, settlement houses and schools to be posted on bulletin boards. A copy of the company magazine was sent to employment agencies with whom Maxwell had established contact.

The results of Maxwell's efforts were gratifying indeed. All five of the objectives defined in top management's initial memorandum had been achieved in substantial measure. Most importantly from an economic viewpoint, the company had avoided any selective patronage pressures. Maxwell's improved standing in the Negro community was illustrated when the local leader of one of the most active Negro groups publicly complimented the company for its progressive employment policy. This feeling was later substantiated by another Negro leader in a personal interview.

Customer reactions continued to bear out the sketchy statistics described in management's original memorandum. Adverse reactions were confined to isolated incidents. And, while the nature of these few complaints made their source more easily identifiable, there appeared to be no statistically significant difference between the performance of white and Negro route-men.

The effects of the new policy on existing white employees were far less troublesome than expected. Negroes found in most cases that within two to four weeks the initial tension and isolation had worked off considerably. Nearly all of them felt natural and well-accepted on the basis of their individual merits within two to six months.

All in all, Maxwell's experience was an exemplary one. There were two areas which might have been improved, however.

The first area concerns the hiring of over-qualified people for jobs. Earlier in this case history, reference was made to the problems caused by filling two route-man positions with Negroes who were not capable of handling the job. Following these occurrences, and very likely because of them, Maxwell adopted the policy of hiring Negroes who were somewhat more than qualified for the position they were initially to fill. It was thought that such a procedure would enable a Negro to master his assigned tasks more quickly, thereby reducing

90

the time required for his acceptance as a competent worker by his associates.

The reasoning is sound, and the philosophy is an effective one when considering "pilot," i.e., initial, placements in a particular plant, division, department, or office. It has a tendency to become self-defeating, however, if applied as a standard, continuous policy. Negroes, like whites, soon become restless when placed in a job that is too easily mastered. They desire to be promoted to more challenging work. To the extent that this desire is not fulfilled, a morale problem results, and the employee may eventually leave the company for a higher-level position elsewhere.

This is precisely what happened at Maxwell. The turnover of newly hired Negroes was considerably greater than that of white employees, due primarily to the offers of greater responsibility and compensation received from other concerns. Top management may have been too reluctant to curtail an initially effective hiring practice when it had served its purpose. A constant sensitivity to the appropriateness of employment policies over time is absolutely essential to the continued success of the over-all program.

The second problem area is related to the degree of decision-making autonomy granted to operating managers in implementing corporate policy. An incident at Maxwell illustrates the importance of this factor.

Through circumstances over which the company had no direct control, a middle-management position in the sales department was vacated on rather short notice. Upon hearing of the new opening, Fred Smith, the director of a local Negro employment agency with which Maxwell had established a firm relationship, suggested that the company consider a Negro named Dick Shanks for the job. Mr. Shanks was a college graduate with some previous business experience. Performance on Maxwell's employment tests and in personal interviews with various management personnel indicated that Mr. Shanks had a pleasant personality and the experience and training necessary to handle the job.

The Maxwell people involved in the interviewing process hesitated to hire Mr. Shanks, because of a repellent though medically correctable facial malformation. Since physical appearance was thought to be important in a sales manager, the Maxwell people felt that medical correction of the deformity was desirable. But it would be relatively expensive and might take a month's time—too long to suit the executive to whom the sales manager reported, who had been handling the added responsibilities of that job since the former incumbent left.

Mr. Smith, the agency director, was asked to participate in the rather lengthy discussion of this touchy issue. The Maxwell personnel finally resolved to inform Mr. Shanks frankly of the problem, and to promise him "every consideration" for a job providing he would first obtain corrective medical attention. As might be expected, someone else was hired for the job, and Mr. Shanks had no further contact with the company.

From Mr. Shank's standpoint, this probably appeared to be nothing more than the run-around Negroes have been receiving for decades from prospective employers. Here was the old "not qualified" argument carried to its extreme, and pretty effectively at that. After all, how many unemployed Negroes are there who would be willing to commit a considerable amount of money (which they probably would not even possess at the time) to beautifying, but nonessential medical attention, solely on the promise that they would receive "every consideration" for some unknown future job? If Maxwell personnel had really wanted to demonstrate their good faith, they might seriously have considered hiring Mr. Shanks first, on the understanding that he would obtain the required medical attention immediately. The company could have solved any money problems by offering to pay for the expenses as they came due, with reimbursement being deducted at a reasonable rate from Mr. Shank's paychecks.

It is impossible to know all the factors which contributed to the company's decision to take the action described above. Two reasons were cited explicitly: 1) the effects of Mr. Shanks' physical problem on his ability to perform the total functions of the job; 2) Mr. Burns' desire to fill the position as expeditiously as possible. It is also possible, though not substantiated, that the executive to whom the job reported was not in sympathy with Maxwell's integration efforts, and was advocating a solution dictated by personal bias. Or, the Maxwell personnel involved may simply not have realized that a request which seemed reasonable to them would not appear so to a Negro.

Whether any or all of these factors influenced Maxwell's decision is not important for our purposes. What _is_ important is that Maxwell's long-standing corporate policy of decentralization of management authority had caused another corporate policy to be compromised at a critical stage of its implementation. If such circumstances are permitted to occur very frequently, it becomes questionable whether any such thing as a "corporate policy" exists in practical fact.

Based on the experiences of other companies with precisely this problem, it is felt that one or both of two solutions might be considered. The first would emphasize stronger central authority with fewer operating decisions being delegated to lower management levels. The second would tend to delegate to all levels the same degree of authority they enjoyed on other operating matters. However, the effective implementation of the policy would be controlled by a very sensitive, frequent reporting procedure backed up by sufficient indications of top management's interest in the program. The gains accruing to a corporation as a result of an active, forward-thinking recruiting and employment policy are too beneficial and hard-won to be subjected to the risks inherent in lax implementation.

# — 8

# PROJECTIONS FOR THE FUTURE

The national unemployment rate for non-white Americans regularly exceeds that for whites. The Manpower Report of the President of March 11, 1963, revealed that in 1962, non-white Americans (90% of whom are Negroes) constituted 11% of the civilian labor force, but 22% of the nation's unemployed. In the first quarter of 1963, 12.7% of the non-white labor force, as compared to 5.7% of the white labor force, was unemployed.

Similarly, nearly two-thirds of the non-whites in the labor force in 1962 were in unskilled jobs, while only one-third of the nation's white workers held comparable positions. In addition, only one-sixth of the non-whites, compared to nearly half of the white working force, maintained white-collar positions.

Estimates of manpower needs for the 1970's indicate that professional and technical jobs requiring a high degree of education and skill will more than double in the next seven years, while, on the other hand, there will be virtually no increase in the demand for unskilled workers. Over the same period, the nation's non-white population is expected to increase by nearly a third. Unless rapid measures are now taken to prepare non-whites for skilled jobs, the United

States will eventually find itself with nearly a quarter of its Negro population unemployed.

In direct correlation will be the continued disparity between Negro and white living standards. A Census Bureau study dated July 31, 1963, showed that in 1962 the Negro male earned, on the average, only 55% as much as his white counterpart. A typical Negro woman earned a little more than half as much as a white woman. The lifetime earnings of a Negro college graduate averaged 47% of those of a white college graduate. And, in 1960, the median income for Negro families was $3,233 as compared to $5,835 for whites.

The discrepancies in job opportunities, living standards, and community life between Negroes and whites in America have been endured in the past by the nation's Negroes largely because they have neither felt nor believed in their own power to force changes in the world in which they lived. But the tenor of the times today is significantly different. Since 1960, the cause of integration has flared into a national phenomenon. It is no longer just the Negro's problem. Despite wide differences of personal opinion among individuals, the official policy of the Federal Government and of an increasing number of public institutions strongly supports active and immediate steps to end the injustices of segregation. The mere fact that public opinion is markedly sensitive to the civil rights question has greatly influenced the new-found courage and dedication of the Negro leaders. In turn, the general tone of the press and the results of public opinion polls indicate that integration as a principle is widely accepted. Its implementation in practical fact is only a matter of time.

Yet, time is precisely the commodity which is most at a premium. The aroused Negro is not willing to wait another fifty years. And, from past experience, he is keenly aware that "official policies" will not in themselves effect integration. The passage of the Civil Rights Bill is no assurance of the efficacy with which it will be enforced. The Supreme Court decision outlawing separate but equal schools was passed in 1954, and there are still many striking cases in which its precepts are not followed. Even the President's Committee on Equal Employment Opportunity is felt by some Negroes to have been largely a token gesture, a feeling which simply serves further to irritate Negro impatience. "If whites choose to procrastinate and rationalize," they say, "we will continue to demonstrate and boycott."

In general it is the opinion of this study that the business community at large has failed to recognize the depth and magnitude of the Negro protest movement. The American businessman has tended to view integration with the sincere but passing concern that he has given to the problems of minority groups in the past. But Negroes today are not concerned with what has or has not been done for other minority groups. They are solely concerned with their own cause and with the injustices which have been peculiar to their lives. And in this singlemindedness, they have found the unity and strength to demand not only equal but often special treatment.

The Negroes' position is enhanced by the fact that it is the nature of our democracy to allow protest movements to develop and to operate freely, so long as they do not impair the basic security of the nation as a whole. That same principle which does not encourage, yet allows, a Southern filibuster in Congress does not encourage, yet tolerates, Negro demonstrations.

But what may be a source of internal strength for the nation at large may prove to be a disaster for a particular institution. Any single company, for example, is seriously vulnerable to the effects of a boycott. The boycott has only begun to be exploited as a tool of the Negro movement. As Negroes become increasingly frustrated in their attempts to obtain satisfaction from politicians and school boards, they will channel more of their energies toward the business community. Reticent companies will be threatened with demonstrations of one kind or another not just once, but continually. And, because of the lack of qualified Negroes, demands will increasingly emphasize scholarships and job training programs. Hopefully, violence will be avoided in the future, but we know now that it can occur in the North as well as in the South. Events of the past summer in New York, New Jersey, and Pennsylvania are proof. Negroes openly admit their willingness to violate existing laws if, in the light of their cause, such violations appear to be either morally or pragmatically justified. They reason that these violations are no more reprehensible and indeed no more illegal than the activities of a company guilty of discrimination. Recalcitrant banks must be prepared to face sit-ins in their lobbies; supermarkets to endure shoppers who fill baskets with food and leave them to spoil; and airline companies to accept the chaos of reservations made but never used.

The Negro movement is in many ways like a new union with which management must learn to cooperate. And this does not by any means suggest that the goals and policies of a business either should or must be compromised. Businessmen are not being bullied, but confronted. They have an opportunity to act with foresight and leadership in a current of change which is irrevocably sweeping the nation. In fact, the very tenor of the Negro movement in the future may be determined by the way in which the business community acknowledges, accepts, and acts to assimilate the Negro protest today.

# APPENDIX

# PLANS FOR PROGRESS PROGRAM

Plans for Progress is a voluntary program to provide leadership in achieving equal employment opportunity.

As a cooperative program of the President's Committee on Equal Employment Opportunity established by Presidential Executive Order, Plans for Progress supplements the federal program applicable to government contractors. Participants are major employers, including companies not involved in government contracting.

## Purpose

The purpose of the program is to achieve progress toward--

Enriching our free society by advancing basic human rights

Providing equal job rights for all Americans

Developing the full potential of our nation's human resources

Reducing the costs to the nation of unemployment, underdevelopment, health and welfare programs, increasing crime and delinquency rates, and deterioration of urban areas

Improving the economic conditions necessary for continuing prosperity, thus increasing the gross national product by many billions of dollars and raising the standard of living

Promoting better community conditions in order to provide an environment for dignity and tranquillity in our daily lives

Contributing through private endeavors toward solution of a major national problem

## Participation in the Program

Participants are leading commercial and industrial companies and educational institutions, with an aggregate of several million employees. Many of these members, prior to joining, had taken positive steps to promote equal employment opportunity and were able to contribute valuable experience in developing the program.

Plans for Progress companies are independent enterprises which participate jointly and voluntarily through this program in the achievement of a common goal.

## Advisory Council on Plans for Progress

The Plans for Progress program was developed in 1961 as an outgrowth of the President's Committee on Equal Employment Opportunity under the chairmanship of the then Vice President Lyndon B. Johnson.

In mid-1963 the Vice President further implemented the program by establishing an Advisory Council to assure greater participation by industry.

The Advisory Council is comprised of 19 industry executives serving staggered three-year terms. The Vice President of the United States, the Secretary of Labor and the Executive Vice Chairman of the President's Committee serve as ex-officio members.

Exhibit 1 (continued)

The Chairman of the Advisory Council is from industry. The Council works through its committees and The Plans for Progress Administrative Staff to develop policies and programs to further the Plans for Progress program.

## Advisory Council Committee

The committees of the Advisory Council, comprised of Council members and other executives from Plans for Progress firms, are:

Communications—Concerned with dissemination of information to and communication with minority groups, employees, the general public and Plans for Progress companies.

Community Relations—Provides guidance and assistance in the development of community conditions and attitudes which promote the implementation of Plans for Progress.

Development—Continues expansion of the Program by recruiting additional participants, and coordinates efforts of local and regional groups.

Employment Resources—Concerned with identification and utilization of applicants for all types and levels of positions.

Research and Information—Collects and disseminates statistical data and functions as a service and evaluating group to the other committees.

Scholarships and Training—Encourages development of programs to improve educational levels and skills to meet the needs of industry.

## Plans for Progress Staff

The Administrative Staff consists of full-time executives on loan from industry to serve in Washington for one year. Their salaries continue to be paid by their respective companies. The Staff functions as an implementation and liaison group for the President's Committee, the Advisory Council and the Plans for Progress program.

## Merits of Plans for Progress

Plans for Progress is a means for communicating policies of equal employment opportunity internally to employees and externally to the community.

It also provides individual participants with a business and industry-wide identification and association with other firms in the program.

Plans for Progress establishes a basis for communication and cooperation with minority groups, other employers, training and recruitment sources, and government agencies.

The exchange of information by member firms through the Advisory Council, its committees and the Washington staff, will benefit all participants by providing an experience base from which to formulate their own decision-making policies for implementing equal employment opportunity.

Exhibit 1 (continued)

Participation

Employers interested in becoming participants in the Plans for Progress program should contact the Administrative Staff. A staff member will assist the company with details and arrangements for joining the program.

Plans for Progress companies are requested to prepare corporate employment figures semi-annually for the first year and annually thereafter. These reports are acccpted by the President's Committee on Equal Employment Opportunity in lieu of compliance reporting for government contractors.*

---

*Plans for Progress Program, Published by the President's Committee on Equal Employment Opportunity.

**Exhibit 1** (continued)

*Examples of Individual Companies' Plans for Progress*

| LOCKHEED AIRCRAFT | PRESIDENT'S COMMITTEE ON |
| CORPORATION | EQUAL EMPLOYMENT OPPORTUNITY |

The President of the United States has stated a national policy that all persons are entitled to equal employment opportunity, regardless of their race, creed, color, or national origin. He has established and charged the President's Committee on Equal Employment Opportunity with responsibility to assist in carrying out this policy.

The Lockheed Aircraft Corporation intends, to the best of its ability, to follow fully this policy as stated by the President, and has voluntarily embarked on a company-wide program to expand and strengthen its efforts to promote equal employment opportunity.

Lockheed has, on forms submitted to it by the President's Committee, attached statistical data on its personnel and responded to questions with regard to its employment policies and practices. All such information was furnished on a completely confidential basis and is only for the official use of the Committee. This information will be used by the Committee as one of the measures of Lockheed's achievements under this Plan for Progress.

The President's Committee is aware that there are many basic factors over which Lockheed has no direct control and which may materially hamper the company's achievement of the Plan for Progress, such as training programs and referral facilities. Therefore, Lockheed will through the President's Committee seek the assistance of public and private agencies in carrying forward its efforts to provide equal employment opportunities.

Lockheed and the President's Committee recognize that this Plan for Progress is a long-range undertaking. In this regard, Lockheed will periodically review (at least once a year) this Plan with the President's Committee. These reviews will be aimed at measuring Lockheed's progress under the Plan. Lockheed recognizes that circumstances may prompt amendments to this Plan in order to better and more rapidly attain the goal of equal employment opportunity.

Undertakings by Lockheed Aircraft Corporation

I. Dissemination of Policy - Implementation
   (A) Lockheed will distribute an up-to-date statement of its non-discrimination policy to all members of management. The statement will be signed by the President of Lockheed, will stress the need for making progress, and will assign responsibility for accomplishing this policy. Divisions and subsidi-

Exhibit 1 (continued)

aries will issue implementing plans. Company policy on the subject will be stated fully in company news periodicals.

II. Recruitment
    (A) Lockheed will in its employment recruitment aggressively seek out more qualified minority group candidates in order to increase the number of employees in many job categories, including but not limited to: professional engineering positions, such as design engineers, mathematicians, associate engineers and draftsmen. Technical positions, such as computer technicians and tabulating analysts. Administrative positions, such as accountants and buyers. Clerical positions, such as stenographers, typists and duplicating operators. Factory operatives, such as machine operators and assemblers.

    (B) Lockheed will advise placement and other officials in colleges from which it recruits that it has a non-discrimination employment policy and will request such officials to refer to it minority group students who appear qualified for employment. Lockheed will work more closely with and make its specific needs known to school counselors and to appropriate local organizations. Lockheed will make certain that state employment offices understand its recruitment policy.

III. Employment, placement and upgrading
    (A) Lockheed will re-analyze its openings for salaried jobs to be certain that all eligible minority group employees have been considered for placement and upgrading. Its Industrial Relations staff, working with other members of management, will re-examine personnel records of minority group employees to make certain that employee skill and potential beyond current job requirements have been properly identified therein for use in filling job openings.

    (B) Lockheed will try to hire for the summer months teachers who are members of minority groups. Such a program has been used for general orientation purposes in the past and should help stimulate a better understanding of industry needs among minority groups. Such employment should help them to secure a better appreciation and awareness of industry needs. Lockheed also will arrange for teachers and student counselors to make plant tours.

IV. Training
Lockheed will:
    (A) Support the inclusion of more qualified minority group members in its apprenticeship program.
    (B) Secure qualified minority group co-op trainees.
    (C) Encourage the establishment of needed vocational training programs and cooperate with school authorities to the great-

Exhibit 1 (continued)

est possible extent in such matters as helping in the determination of course content and furnishing competent instructors and will, in addition, encourage participation of minority group employees in such vocational programs.

(D) Encourage participation of minority group employees in company-sponsored training programs, such as career development training, home study courses and work-study plans.

(E) Make certain that qualified minority group employees are included in supervisory and pre-supervisory training classes and in other classes offered to employees on company time.

V. Transfer and layoff
(A) Lockheed will review the transfer, layoff, and other termination procedures to insure that they are non-discriminatory in operation.

VI. General
Lockheed will:
(A) Maintain all facilities such as eating facilities, rest rooms and recreation facilities on a non-segregated basis.
(B) Encourage the employee recreation and management clubs to formalize their non-discrimination policies and to insure that they are carried out.
(C) Institute periodic checks (not less frequently than quarterly) to insure that the policy and objectives stated herein are being carried out.

VII. Implementation
It is recognized that the objectives herein may not be carried out at a uniform rate or manner throughout the company because of a number of factors, for example:
1. Some segments of the company will be expanding and therefore have more opportunities to employ minority group personnel.
2. Where layoffs have occurred, those employees laid off or downgraded have certain priorities under company policy and collective bargaining agreements. Generally, laid-off employees must first be hired before consideration can be given to new employees.

Undertakings by the President's Committee on Equal Employment Opportunity

I. Recruiting
The Committee will:
(A) Request the United States Department of Labor to assign personnel to work with the appropriate state employment services to review and intensify efforts to obtain applicants

Exhibit 1 (continued)

for referral to Lockheed without regard to race, creed, color or national origin.

(B) Solicit the support of appropriate specialized community agencies to assist recruiting efforts under this Plan for Progress.

II. Training
The Committee will
(A) Request the Bureau of Apprenticeship and Training of the U.S. Department of Labor to encourage and promote the selection for apprenticeship training of applicants without regard to race, creed, color or national origin.
(B) Request the U.S. Department of Health, Education and Welfare to review, encourage and strengthen counseling and guidance services in school systems. That Department will be asked to assign personnel to encourage participation of persons in minority groups in its vocational education programs. In addition, it will be asked to develop new programs aimed at the encouragement of cooperative efforts between educational facilities and employers as to this program.

III. Labor liaison
The Committee will:
(A) Work cooperatively with the International Association of Machinists and all other appropriate unions, at both the local and national levels, in reviewing and supporting constructive action on problems connected with apprenticeship training, transfer procedures and seniority rights where union action may be helpful.

IV. Contracting agency

The Committee will work with the Department of the Air Force and other contracting agencies to assist Lockheed and the Committee in coordination and follow-through on their undertakings under this Plan for Progress. The contracting agencies will be requested to make continuing evaluation and progress reports available to the Committee and Lockheed.

V. General
(A) Lockheed will report to the Committee any difficulties encountered by it in achieving this Plan for Progress in those instances where it reasonably believes the services of the Committee can be materially constructive in overcoming them.
(B) With regard to the annual review of progress contemplated in this plan, it is not intended that specific numerical targets or goals shall be set. Nonetheless, it is intended that evaluation will be made, in part, in terms of increases in the numbers of minority persons hired, promoted, involved in train-

**Exhibit 1** (continued

ing and occupying responsible positions within the Corporation.

Lockheed Aircraft Corporation

By: /s/ Courtlandt S. Gross
_____
President

Date: May 25, 1961

President's Committee on
Equal Employment Opportunity

By: /s/ Lyndon B. Johnson
_____

Vice President of the
United States

*     *     *     *     *

### THE SHERWIN-WILLIAMS COMPANY
### "PLANS FOR PROGRESS" PREAMBLE

Our Government's policy regarding equal employment opportunity
has been clearly stated by the President. To augment this policy and
to provide leadership among industry in achieving equal employment
opportunity, Plans for Progress, a voluntary program, has been established. Participants in the Plans for Progress are major employers--
primarily, though not exclusively, those in the defense industries.

The purpose of the program as stated by the Plans for Progress
Advisory Council is "to achieve progress toward--

Enriching our free society by advancing basic human rights

Providing equal job rights for all Americans

Developing the full potential of our nation's human resources

Reducing the costs to the nation of unemployment, underdevelopment, health and welfare programs,...crime and delinquency,..
and deterioration of urban areas

Improving the economic conditions necessary for continuing
prosperity, thus increasing the gross national product by many
billions of dollars and raising the standard of living

Promoting better community conditions in order to provide an
environment for dignity and tranquillity in our daily lives

Contributing through private endeavors toward solution of a major
national problem."

The Sherwin-Williams Company has voluntarily offered to join the
nation's leading industries in this program, and in so doing has committed itself to a full share of responsibility for carrying out the
above stated purposes.

Exhibit 1 (continued)

There are several important reasons why the Sherwin-Williams Company has voluntarily accepted this major responsibility:

First, aside from the fact that equal opportunity is a basic premise on which our nation was founded, there is a strong moral persuasion that constantly urges us to support the proposition that everyone, regardless of race, creed, color or national origin, is entitled to an equal opportunity to seek a better way of life.

Secondly, we are not unmindful of our many friends from every race, creed, color and national origin whose use of our products has contributed to our remarkable growth.

Thirdly, our many long service employees from the various minority groups have not only appreciated their opportunities with the Sherwin-Williams Company, but also have demonstrated their ability and desire to perform competitively.

Finally, and of great importance, we believe that participating in the Plans for Progress program would be in keeping with the wishes of our employees. Our own earlier steps in this direction--the employment of several hundred minority group employees in both hourly and salaried jobs—has been fully accepted by Sherwin-Williams personnel. More recently, the wholehearted cooperation by all levels of management as well as by fellow employees in our own "positive action" program has made it possible for the Company to substantially increase the number of minority group personnel in key jobs without the incidents that have often accompanied integration of such personnel. Our experience in this voluntary program assures us that our people understand the continued commitments in our proposed Plan for Progress and the responsibility attached to it and that we are ready for participation in the Plans for Progress program.

### Plans for Progress Agreement

The Sherwin-Williams Company has joined the President's Committee on Equal Employment Opportunity in the following agreed statement on a Plan for Progress:

## UNDERTAKINGS BY THE SHERWIN-WILLIAMS COMPANY

I.  Statement of Policy

It is the policy of The Sherwin-Williams Company that applicants for employment are recruited, selected and hired on the basis of individual merit and ability with respect to positions being filled and potential for promotions or transfers which may be expected to develop. Applicants are to be recruited, selected, and hired without discrimination because of race, creed, color, or national origin.

Personnel procedures and practices with regard to training, promotion, transfer, compensation, demotion, layoff, or termi-

Exhibit 1 (continued)

nation are to be administered with due consideration to job performance, experience and qualifications, and there shall be no discrimination because of race, creed, color, or national origin.

## II. Communication of Policy

The Company's policy has been issued to all managerial personnel responsible for employee relations at all domestic facilities of the Company. It will continue to issue statements of this policy as often as necessary to insure effective compliance at all points.

The Company will also publicize this Plan for Progress commitment in its various publications and distribute copies for the information and guidance of managerial personnel in all domestic facilities.

## III. Responsibility for Employment Policy Enforcement

General responsibility for the implementation of the Company's employment policies has been assigned to the Industrial Relations Department.

All Managers will be responsible for the continuance of the Company's nondiscrimination policy in their respective units.

## IV. Recruitment and Placement

College placement offices and public and private employment agencies which have been sources of job applicants have been notified of the Company's equal employment opportunity policy and new sources of applicants will be so notified as they develop. The Company will continue to use and seek other reliable sources that furnish referrals from minority groups. The Company's recruiting practice will continue to be the employment of those best qualified for the job openings and who have the greatest potential for advancement, without regard to race, creed, color and national origin.

## V. Transfer, Promotion and Layoff

Job reassignments and layoffs will continue to be related to job performance, experience and qualifications, with due regard to service with the Company. In keeping with the Company's policy on equal employment opportunity, job assignments will be made without regard to race, creed, color and national origin.

The provisions of collective bargaining agreements concerning transfers, promotions, demotions and layoffs will be administered free of discrimination because of race, creed, color and national origin.

Exhibit 1 (continued)

## VI. Training Programs

All Company training programs including those for new employees, apprenticeship and other on-the-job training, management development and scholastic opportunities will be made available on the basis of Company need, individual qualifications and ability, without regard to race, creed, color and national origin.

## VII. Facilities

The Company's facilities for personnel including cafeterias, lockers, showers and rest rooms shall continue to be available to all employees on a nondiscriminatory basis.

## VIII. Reporting

The Company will furnish the Committee information at least annually for confidential use by the Committee as an aid in measuring the success and the progress of the Company's efforts in implementing its "Plan for Progress."

## UNDERTAKINGS BY THE PRESIDENT'S COMMITTEE ON EQUAL EMPLOYMENT OPPORTUNITY

### I. Recruiting

The Committee will:

A. Continue to work with the United States Department of Labor's employment specialists to cooperate with the appropriate State Employment Services in reviewing and intensifying efforts to obtain qualified applicants for referral to The Sherwin-Williams Company without regard to race, creed, color or national origin.

B. Upon request, solicit the support of appropriate specialized community agencies to assist recruiting efforts under this Plan for Progress.

### II. Training

The Committee will work with the U.S. Department of Health, Education and Welfare in reviewing, encouraging and strengthening counseling and guidance services in school systems where The Sherwin-Williams Company has major operations. That Department has assigned personnel to encourage participation of persons in minority groups in its vocational education programs. In addition, new programs are being developed aimed

Exhibit 1 (continued)

at the encouragement of cooperative efforts between educational facilities, community agencies and employers as to this program.

III.  Labor Liaison

The Committee will work cooperatively with appropriate unions, at both the local and national levels, in reviewing and supporting constructive action on problems connected with apprenticeship training, transfer procedures and seniority rights where union action may be useful.

IV.  Contracting Agencies

The Committee will work with the appropriate contracting agencies to assist The Sherwin-Williams Company and the Committee in coordination and follow-through on their undertakings under this Plan for Progress.

V.  General

The Sherwin-Williams Company officials should feel free to report to the Committee any difficulties encountered in achieving this Plan for Progress in those instances where it is reasonably believed services of the Committee can be materially constructive in overcoming them.

THE SHERWIN-WILLIAMS COMPANY

The President's Committee on Equal Employment Opportunity

By:_____
     President

By:_____
     Lyndon B. Johnson
     President of the
     United States

\*    \*    \*    \*    \*

An Example of a Community Plan

MILWAUKEE EMPLOYERS VOLUNTARY PLAN
FOR EQUAL EMPLOYMENT OPPORTUNITY

The Milwaukee Voluntary Employment Opportunity Council was formed on December 16, 1963, to implement a voluntary plan designed to cope with employment problems of Negroes and other minority groups in the Milwaukee area.

The complete text of the MILWAUKEE EMPLOYERS VOLUNTARY

Exhibit 1 (continued)

PLAN FOR EQUAL EMPLOYMENT OPPORTUNITY providing for the establishment of the Council is set forth below.

I. Milwaukee Minority Group Employment Problems

The recognized problems of Milwaukee minority groups relate to the areas of (a) employment (b) housing and (c) education. The underlying problem is economic and hence solution of the employment problem is basic to the solution of the other problems.

For example, there is a much higher rate of unemployment among Negroes than other citizen groups in the Milwaukee community. Employed Negroes are concentrated in lower job classifications and relatively few are found in the skilled—clerical—technical—professional classifications. Thus larger numbers are found on public relief rolls and have lower income status than among other citizen groups.

Many Milwaukee Negroes and other minority group members indicate they have been discouraged from preparing for full employment qualification or aspiring to upgraded employment status because of assumed employment discrimination on account of race, color, religion or national origin. This is believed to be a contributing factor to the minority group unemployment and under-employment problem and is a matter of direct employer interest and concern. Over the years progress has been made in the elimination of employment discrimination, but it is evident that further affirmative action is required in the light of current community circumstances.

It is a first essential to solution of minority group employment problems that it become an established, known fact throughout the entire Milwaukee community that there is no employment discrimination on account of race, color, religion, or national origin. This assurance and realization is needed motivation to prepare for full employment qualification.

And beyond that it is also essential that continuing employer interest and attention be directed to solution of other related minority group employment problems that may arise from time to time.

II. Basic Objectives of the Voluntary Plan

The basic objectives of this proposed voluntary plan are to
a) make certain that there is no employment discrimination in the Milwaukee community on account of race, color, religion or national origin;
b) persuade all Milwaukee area employers to affirm this purpose and to openly support the principle and practice of non-discriminatory hiring, promotion, training, and compensation of employes on the basis of individual qualification and merit;
c) convincingly communicate to the Milwaukee Negro community and other minority groups, the willingness of Milwaukee employers to hire qualified Negro and other minority group applicants and the availability of jobs, and thus establish a community knowl-

**Exhibit 1** (continued)

edge that attaining of essential qualifications leads directly to
equal employment opportunity;
d) directly encourage Negroes and members of other minority
groups to obtain the necessary education and training to qualify
for existing and future jobs and to aspire to upgraded employment status; and
e) establish a systematic method of assembling and disseminating
data and information among Milwaukee area employers relating
to minority group employment and progress made in achieving
plan objectives.

III. Implementation of Voluntary Plan

Participating Milwaukee employers who have not already done so
will take the following confirming action to effectively implement this
plan—
a) adopt a written policy of nondiscrimination with respect to race,
color, religion and national origin of job applicants and employes
in hiring, promotion, training and compensation and other pertinent areas of employment;
b) impress upon employment and supervisory personnel the responsibility of insuring compliance with the provisions of the non-
discriminatory policy;
c) in recruiting of employes
(1) include in all employment ads the phrase "an equal opportunity employer";
(2) advise all recruiting sources of the existence of the non-
discriminatory employment policy and desire to interview all
qualified applicants;
(3) establish contact with the Milwaukee Urban League and other
organizations and agencies having special knowledge of the
availability of qualified Negro and other minority group job
applicants;
d) participate in other programs and activities designed to promote
minority group knowledge of Milwaukee business community and
employment opportunities such as—plant tours—school career
days—school co-op and summer employment programs.

IV. Milwaukee Voluntary Equal Employment Opportunity Council

To provide an operating structure to advise and assist participating
employers, and other Milwaukee area employers indicating interest in
participating in the plan, and to consider Negro and other minority
group employment problems that arise from time to time—
a) there is hereby established a MILWAUKEE VOLUNTARY EQUAL
EMPLOYMENT OPPORTUNITY COUNCIL comprised of the chief
executives of all interested Milwaukee area employers;
b) the council shall elect a Board of Directors, comprised of fifteen
council members to act as a governing body, five to serve a term

114

Exhibit 1 (continued)

of one year, five to serve a term of two years, and five to serve
a term of three years, and annually thereafter five for full three
year terms replacing directors whose terms expire;
c) the Board of Directors shall elect a chairman annually to serve
a term of one year and appoint an ADVISORY COMMITTEE of
twelve qualified employer representatives to serve at the pleas-
ure of the Board;
d) the advisory committee shall be authorized to
(1) establish appropriate subcommittees to consider and report
to the Board of Directors and the council on various aspects
of the Negro and other minority group employment problems
such as education and training,
(2) propose solutions to problems and develop recommended
programs,
(3) advise and counsel interested Milwaukee area employers considering participation in the plan,
(4) perform such other functions as may be assigned by the
Board of Directors from time to time,
(5) designate a member to act as chairman and, subject to ap-
proval of the Board of Directors, select a Secretary to serve
the council, the committee and the Board of Directors.
e) The Board of Directors shall take such other action as in their
judgment may be deemed necessary or appropriate to facilitate
administration, and effectuate the purposes, of the plan.

V. Establishment of "Milwaukee Skills Bank"

The Council will cooperate with the Milwaukee Urban League in its
plan to establish a "Milwaukee Skills Bank" for the purpose of serving
as a clearinghouse for exchange of information on availability of qualified job applicants and available jobs and required job skills.

Adopted December 16, 1963

## Exhibit 2
### NEGRO NEWSPAPERS IN THE UNITED STATES

ALABAMA

| | |
|---|---|
| Birmingham | World |
| Montgomery | Tribune |

CALIFORNIA

| | |
|---|---|
| Los Angeles | Eagle |
| | Herald-Dispatch |
| | Sentinel |
| Oakland | California Voice |
| San Diego | Lighthouse |
| San Francisco | Bay Area Independent |
| | Sun Reporter |

COLORADO

| | |
|---|---|
| Denver | Blade |

DISTRICT OF COLUMBIA

| | |
|---|---|
| Washington | Afro-American |

FLORIDA

| | |
|---|---|
| Ft. Lauderdale | Spur |
| Jacksonville | Florida Star |
| Miami | Times |
| Tampa-St. Petersburg | Sentinel Bulletin |
| | News Reporter |
| West Palm Beach | The Photo News |

GEORGIA

| | |
|---|---|
| Albany | Southwest Georgian |
| Atlanta | Daily World |
| | Inquirer |
| Savannah | Herald |
| | Tribune |

ILLINOIS

| | |
|---|---|
| Chicago | Courier |
| | Defender |
| | New Crusader |

INDIANA

| | |
|---|---|
| Gary | American |
| Indianapolis | Indiana Herald |
| | Recorder |

116

Exhibit 2 (continued)

IOWA

    Des Moines                  Bystander

KANSAS

    Wichita                      Enlightener

KENTUCKY

    Louisville                 Defender

LOUISIANA

    Baton Rouge           News Leader
    New Orleans           Louisiana Weekly
    Shreveport             Sun

MARYLAND

    Baltimore               Afro-American

MASSACHUSETTS

    Boston                    Graphic
                                Citizen

MICHIGAN

    Detroit                    Courier
                                Michigan Chronicle

MINNESOTA

    Minneapolis           Spokesman
    St. Paul               Recorder

MISSISSIPPI

    Jackson                   Advocate

MISSOURI

    Kansas City           Call
    St. Louis              Argus

NEBRASKA

    Omaha                     Star

NEW JERSEY

    Asbury Park           Central Jersey Post
    Newark                    Afro-American
                                Herald News

Exhibit 2 (continued)

NEW YORK

| | |
|---|---|
| Corona | East Elmhurst News and Queens Voice |
| Hastings-on-Hudson | Westchester City Press |
| New York | Amsterdam News |
| | Courier |
| Rochester | The American Negro |

NORTH CAROLINA

| | |
|---|---|
| Charlotte | Post |
| Durham | Carolina Times |
| Greensboro | Future Outlook |
| Raleigh | Carolinian |
| Wilmington | Journal |

OHIO

| | |
|---|---|
| Akron | Ohio Informer |
| Cleveland | Call and Post |
| | Courier |
| Columbus | Ohio Sentinel |

OKLAHOMA

| | |
|---|---|
| Tulsa | Oklahoma Eagle |

PENNSYLVANIA

| | |
|---|---|
| Philadelphia | Afro-American |
| | Courier |
| | Independent |
| | Tribune |
| Pittsburgh | Courier |

TENNESSEE

| | |
|---|---|
| Chattanooga | Observer |
| Memphis | Tri-State Defender |
| | World |

TEXAS

| | |
|---|---|
| Dallas | Express |
| | Post Tribune |
| Ft. Worth | Mind |
| Houston | Informer |
| San Antonio | Register |

VIRGINIA

| | |
|---|---|
| Charlottesville | Tribune |
| Norfolk-Portsmouth | Journal and Guide |

Exhibit 2 (continued)

VIRGINIA (continued)

    Richmond                             Afro-American
    Roanoke                              Tribune

WISCONSIN

    Milwaukee                          Defender

Agent for many of the listed newspapers:

    AMALGAMATED PUBLISHERS, INC
    310 Madison Avenue
    New York, New York
            and
    166 West Washington Street
    Chicago 2, Illinois

Exhibit 3

# NEGRO PROGRAM RADIO STATIONS IN THE UNITED STATES

ALABAMA

| | |
|---|---|
| Birmingham | WENN |
| | WJLD |
| | WJLN(FM) |
| Demopolis | WXAL |
| Eufala | WULA |
| Huntsville | WEUP |
| Jasper | WARF |
| Marion | WJAM |
| Mobile | WMOZ |
| | WGOK |
| Montgomery | WRMA |
| Opelika | WJHO |
| Selma | WGWC |
| Tuscaloosa | WTUG |

ARIZONA

| | |
|---|---|
| Phoenix | KCAC |

ARKANSAS

| | |
|---|---|
| Little Rock | KOKY |
| Pine Bluff | KPBA |
| Warren | KWRF |

CALIFORNIA

| | |
|---|---|
| Inglewood | KTYM(FM) |
| Los Angeles | KGFJ |
| San Francisco | KDIA |
| Santa Monica | KDAY |

DISTRICT OF COLUMBIA

| | |
|---|---|
| Washington | WOOK |
| | WUST |

FLORIDA

| | |
|---|---|
| Daytona Beach | WELE |
| Jacksonville | WRHC |
| Miami | WFEC |
| Miami Beach | WMBM |
| Ocala | WKOS |
| Pensacola | WBOP |
| Tampa | WIOK |
| | WTMP |
| Tampa-St. Petersburg | WYOU |

Exhibit 3 (continued)

FLORIDA (continued)

| | |
|---|---|
| West Palm Beach | WIRK |
| Winter Garden | WOKB |

GEORGIA

| | |
|---|---|
| Albany | WALG |
| Americus | WDEC |
| Atlanta | WAOK |
| | WERD |
| Augusta | WAUG |
| Buford | WDMF |
| Cairo | WGRA |
| Carrollton | WLBB |
| Columbus | WCLS |
| | WOKS |
| Dawson | WDWD |
| Macon | WIBB |
| Montezuma | WMNZ |
| North Augusta | WTHB |
| Sandersville | WSNT |
| Statesboro | WWNS |
| Tifton | WTIF |
| Valdosta | WGOV |

ILLINOIS

| | |
|---|---|
| Chicago | WAAF |
| | WSBC |
| Oak Park | WOPA |

INDIANA

| | |
|---|---|
| Gary | WWCA |
| Hammond | WJOB |

KENTUCKY

| | |
|---|---|
| Hopkinsville | WKOF(FM) |
| Louisville | WLOU |
| Paducah | WKYB |
| Pineville | WMLF |

LOUISIANA

| | |
|---|---|
| Alexandria | KALB |
| Baton Rouge | WXOK |
| Lafayette | KVOL |
| Monroe | KLIC |
| New Iberia | KANE |
| New Orleans | WBOK |

Exhibit 3 (continued)

LOUISIANA (continued)

| | |
|---|---|
| New Orleans | WMRY |
| | WWEZ |
| | WYLD |
| Opelousas | KSLO |
| Shreveport | KOKA |

MARYLAND

| | |
|---|---|
| Annapolis | WANN |
| Baltimore | WEBB |
| | WWIN |
| Bethesda | WUST |

MASSACHUSETTS

| | |
|---|---|
| Boston | WILD |

MICHIGAN

| | |
|---|---|
| Detroit | WCHB |
| | WCHD(FM) |
| | WJLB |
| Flint | WAMM |

MISSISSIPPI

| | |
|---|---|
| Clarksdale | WROX |
| Greenville | WGVM |
| Hattiesburg | WXXX |
| Indianola | WDLT |
| Jackson | WOKJ |
| Laurel | WLAU |
| Leland | WESY |
| Macon | WMBC |
| Meridian | WQIC |
| Starkville | WSSO |
| West Point | WROB |

MISSOURI

| | |
|---|---|
| Kansas City | KPRS |
| St. Louis | KATZ |

NEW JERSEY

| | |
|---|---|
| Newark | WHBI(FM) |
| | WNJR |

NEW YORK

| | |
|---|---|
| Buffalo | WUFO |
| New York | WWRL |

Exhibit 3 (continued)

NORTH CAROLINA

| Durham | WSRC |
| Greensboro | WEAL |
| | WGBG |
| High Point | WHPE |
| Kinston | WELS |
| Shelby | WADA |
| Williamston | WIAM |
| Winston-Salem | WAAA |

OHIO

| Cincinnati | WCIN |
| Cleveland | WABQ |

OKLAHOMA

| Muskogee | KBIX |

OREGON

| Sand Springs | KTOW |

PENNSYLVANIA

| Pittsburgh | WAMO |
| Philadelphia | WDAS |

SOUTH CAROLINA

| Charleston | WPAL |
| Columbia | WOIC |
| Florence | WYNN |
| Greenville | WESC |
| Hampton | WBHC |
| Hartsville | WHSC |
| Kingstree | WDKD |
| St. George | WQIZ |
| Spartanburg | WZOO |

TENNESSEE

| Chattanooga | WMFS |
| | WNOO |
| Clarksville | WJZM |
| Jackson | WJAK |
| Memphis | WDIA |
| | WLOK |
| Nashville | WLAC |
| | WSOK |
| | WVOL |

Exhibit 3 (continued)

TEXAS

| | |
|---|---|
| Beaumont | KJET |
| Fort Worth | KNOK |
| Houston | KCOH |
| | KYOK |
| Longview | KLUE |
| Marshall | KMHT |
| San Antonio | KCOR |
| Tyler | KDOK |

VIRGINIA

| | |
|---|---|
| Danville | WILA |
| Franklin | WYSR |
| Gloucester | WDDY |
| Norfolk | WRAP |

WASHINGTON

| | |
|---|---|
| Seattle | WZAM(FM) |

WEST VIRGINIA

| | |
|---|---|
| Bluefield | WKOY |

WISCONSIN

| | |
|---|---|
| Milwaukee | WAWA |


Agent for many of the listed stations:

BERNARD HOWARD AND COMPANY, INC.
20 East 46th Street
New York 17, New York
         and
35 East Wacker Drive
Chicago 1, Illinois
         and
1401 Peachtree Street, N.E.
Atlanta, Georgia
         and
8430 Santa Monica Blvd.
Los Angeles 69, California
         and
58 Sutter Street
San Francisco 4, California

## Exhibit 4

## PREDOMINANTLY NEGRO COLLEGES AND UNIVERSITIES

| School and Location | Support | Enrollment | Type | |
|---|---|---|---|---|
| ALABAMA | Senior Colleges | | | |
| Alabama Agricultural and Mechanical College(a) Normal | State | 1265 | CE | |
| Alabama College(a) Montevallo | State | 1200 | CE | |
| Miles College(a) Birmingham | CME | 827 | CE | BA |
| Oakwood College(a) Huntsville | SDA | 270 | CE | |
| Selma University Selma | Bapt | | | |
| Stillman College(a) Tuscaloosa | Presby | 463 | CE | |
| Talladega College(a) Talladega | AMA, UNCF | 382 | CE | |
| Tuskegee Institute(a) Tuskegee | Ind, UNCF | 2152 | CE | Eng |
| | Junior Colleges | | | |
| Alabama Lutheran Academy Selma | ELC | | | |
| Daniel Payne College(ja) Birmingham | AME | 210 | CE | |
| Lomax-Hannon College Greenville | AMEZ | | | |
| ARKANSAS | Senior Colleges | | | |
| Arkansas Agricultural and Mechanical College(a) College Heights | State | 999 | CE | BA |
| Arkansas Agricultural, Mechanical and Normal College(a) Pine Bluff | State | 1469 | CE | |
| Arkansas Baptist College(b) Little Rock | Bapt | 250 | CE | |
| Philander Smith College(a) Little Rock | Meth, UNCF | 732 | CE | BA |
| | Junior Colleges | | | |
| Shorter College(jb) North Little Rock | AME | 183 | CE | |

Exhibit 4 (continued)

| School and Location | Support | Enrollment | Type |
|---|---|---|---|
| DELAWARE | Senior Colleges | | |
| Delaware State College(a)<br>  Dover | State | 350 | CE BA |
| DISTRICT OF COLUMBIA | Senior Colleges | | |
| District of Columbia<br>  Teachers College(a)<br>    Washington | Munic. | 1431 | CE |
| Howard University(a)<br>  Washington | Pvt | 6507 | CE BA,<br> Eng |
| FLORIDA | Senior Colleges | | |
| Bethune-Cookman<br>  College(a)<br>    Daytona Beach | Meth, UNCF | 699 | CE BA |
| Florida Agricultural and<br>  Mechanical University(a)<br>    Tallahassee | State | 2962 | CE |
| Florida Normal and Indus-<br>  trial Memorial College(a)<br>    St. Augustine | Bapt | 294 | CE |
| | Junior Colleges | | |
| Gibbs Junior College(jb)<br>  St. Petersburg | Public | 647 | CE |
| Howard Junior College<br>  Ocala | Public | | |
| Roosevelt Junior<br>  College(jb)<br>    West Palm Beach | Public | 180 | CE |
| Rosenwald Community<br>  Junior College(jb)<br>    Panama City | Public | 53 | CE |
| Suwannee River Junior<br>  College(jb)<br>    Madison | Public | | CE |
| Volusia County Community<br>  College (jb)<br>    Daytona Beach | Public | 169 | CE |
| Washington Junior<br>  College(jb)<br>    Pensacola | County | 188 | CE |
| Edward Waters College(ja)<br>  Jacksonville | AME | 628 | CE |

**Exhibit 4** (continued)

| School and Location | Support | Enrollment | Type |
|---|---|---|---|
| GEORGIA | Senior Colleges | | |
| Albany State College(a) Albany | State | 842 | CE |
| Atlanta University(a) (graduate school only) Atlanta | Pvt | 4032 | CE |
| Clark College(a) Atlanta | Meth, UNCF | 878 | CE |
| Fort Valley State College(a) Fort Valley | State | 1009 | CE |
| Interdenominational Theological Center Atlanta | Interd | 115 | CE |
| Morehouse College(a) Atlanta | Bapt, UNCF | 796 | M   BA |
| Morris Brown College(a) Atlanta | AME, UNCF | 849 | CE |
| Paine College(a) Augusta | Meth, CME, UNCF | 373 | CE |
| Savannah State College(a) Savannah | State | 1126 | CE   BA |
| Spelman College(a) Atlanta | Bapt, UNCF | 500 | F |
| ILLINOIS | Junior Colleges | | |
| Chicago City Junior College, Crane Branch(ja) Chicago | City | 1922 | CE |
| Chicago City Junior College, Woodrow Wilson Branch(ja) Chicago | City | 2801 | CE |
| KENTUCKY | Senior Colleges | | |
| Kentucky State College(a) Frankfort | State | 591 | CE   BA |
| LOUISIANA | Senior Colleges | | |
| Dillard University(a) New Orleans | AMA, Meth, UNCF | 904 | CE |
| Grambling College(a) Grambling | Public | 2657 | CE |
| Leland College(b) Baker | Bapt | 171 | CE |

Exhibit 4 (continued)

| School and Location | Support | Enrollment | Type |
|---|---|---|---|
| LOUISIANA (continued) | Senior Colleges | | |
| Southern University and Agricultural and Mechanical College(a) Scotlandville | State | 4791 | CE Eng |
| Xavier University of Louisiana(a) New Orleans | RC, UNCF | 825 | CE |
| MARYLAND | Senior Colleges | | |
| Choppin State Teachers College(b) Baltimore | State | 287 | CE |
| Maryland State College(a) Princess Anne | State | 472 | CE |
| Morgan State College(a) Baltimore | State | 2455 | CE |
| State Teachers College at Bowie(b) Bowie | State | 350 | CE |
| | Junior Colleges | | |
| George Washington Carver Junior College Rockville | Pvt | | |
| MISSISSIPPI | Senior Colleges | | |
| Alcorn Agricultural and Mechanical College(a) Port Gibson | Public | 944 | CE |
| Jackson State College(a) Jackson | State | 1738 | CE |
| Mississippi Industrial College(b) Holly Springs | CME | 550 | CE |
| Mississippi Vocational College(b) Itta Bena | State | 954 | CE |
| Rust College(b) Holly Springs | Meth | 502 | CE |
| Tougaloo Southern Christian College(a) Tougaloo | AMA, UNCF, D. of C. | 509 | CE |

Exhibit 4 (continued)

| School and Location | Support | Enrollment | Type |
|---|---|---|---|
| **MISSISSIPPI** (continued) | Junior Colleges | | |
| J. P. Campbell College(jb) Jackson | AME | 144 | CE |
| Coahoma Junior College(jb) Clarksdale | Public | 343 | CE |
| Mary Holmes Junior College(jb) West Point | Pres | 133 | CE |
| Okolona College(jb) Okolona | PE | 200 | CE |
| Piney Woods Junior College(jb) Piney Woods | Ind. | 112 | CE |
| Prentiss Normal and Industrial Institute(jb) Prentiss | Ind. | 80 | CE |
| Utica Junior College(jb) Utica | County | 367 | CE |
| **MISSOURI** | Senior Colleges | | |
| Lincoln University(a) Jefferson City | State | 1489 | CE BA |
| **NORTH CAROLINA** | Senior Colleges | | |
| Agricultural and Technical College(a) Greensboro | State | 2914 | CE BA, Eng |
| Barber-Scotia College(a) Concord | Pres, UNCF | | CE |
| Bennett College(a) Greensboro | Meth, UNCF | 542 | F |
| Elizabeth City State Teachers College(a) Elizabeth City | State | 669 | CE |
| Fayetteville State Teachers College(a) Fayetteville | State | 834 | CE |
| Johnson C. Smith University(a) Charlotte | Pres, UNCF | 881 | CE |
| Livingstone College(a) Salisbury | AMEZ, UNCF | 564 | CE |
| North Carolina College at Durham(a) Durham | State | 2129 | CE BA |

Exhibit 4 (continued)

| School and Location | Support | Enrollment | Type |
|---|---|---|---|
| NORTH CAROLINA (continued) | Senior Colleges | | |
| St. Augustine's College(a) Raleigh | PE, UNCF | 477 | CE |
| Shaw University(a) Raleigh | Bapt, UNCF, Ind | 574 | CE |
| Winston-Salem Teachers College(a) Winston-Salem | State | 912 | CE |
| Carver College(jb) Charlotte | Public | 261 | CE |
| Immanuel Lutheran Greensboro | ELC | | |
| Kittrell College Kittrell | AME | | |
| OHIO | Senior Colleges | | |
| Central State College(a) Wilberforce | State | 1704 | CE BA, Eng |
| Wilberforce University Wilberforce | AME | 350 | CE |
| OKLAHOMA | Senior Colleges | | |
| Langston University(a) Langston | State | 550 | CE |
| PENNSYLVANIA | Senior Colleges | | |
| Cheyney State Teachers College(a) Cheyney | State | 800 | CE |
| Lincoln University(a) Lincoln University | Ind, UNCF | 370 | M |
| SOUTH CAROLINA | Senior Colleges | | |
| Allen University(a) Columbia | AME | 1133 | CE |
| Benedict College(a) Columbia | Bapt, UNCF | 823 | CE |
| Claflin University(a) Orangeburg | Meth | 378 | CE |
| Morris College(b) Sumter | Bapt | 450 | CE |
| South Carolina State College(a) Orangeburg | State | 2113 | CE BA |

130

Exhibit 4 (continued)

| School and Location | Support | Enrollment | Type |
|---|---|---|---|
| SOUTH CAROLINA (continued) | Junior Colleges | | |
| Clinton Junior College(jb) Rock Hill | AMEZ | 69 | CE |
| Friendship Junior College(jb) Rock Hill | Bapt | 180 | CE |
| Mather Junior College Beaufort | Bapt | | |
| Voorhees School and Junior College(ja) Denmark | PE | 185 | CE |
| TENNESSEE | Senior Colleges | | |
| Fisk University(a) Nashville | Ind, UNCF | 842 | CE Eng |
| Knoxville College(a) Knoxville | Pres, UNCF | 513 | CE |
| Lane College(a) Jackson | CME, UNCF | 540 | CE |
| LeMoyne College(a) Memphis | AMA, UNCF | 551 | CE |
| Meharry Medical College Nashville | Pvt | 412 | CE |
| Tennessee Agricultural and Industrial State University(a) Nashville | State | 3251 | CE BA, Eng |
| | Junior Colleges | | |
| Morristown College(ja) Morristown | Meth | 200 | CE |
| Owen College(ja) Memphis | Bapt | 259 | CE |
| TEXAS | Senior Colleges | | |
| Bishop College(a) Marshall | Bapt, UNCF | 558 | CE |
| Butler College(b) Tyler | Bapt | 204 | CE |
| Huston-Tillotson College(a) Austin | Meth, AMA, UNCF | 438 | CE |
| Jarvis Christian College(a) Hawkins | D. of C. | 326 | CE |

Exhibit 4 (continued)

| School and Location | Support | Enrollment | Type |
|---|---|---|---|
| TEXAS (continued) | Senior Colleges | | |
| Mary Allen College(b) | | | |
| Crockett | Bapt | | CE |
| Paul Quinn(b) | | | |
| Waco | AME | 326 | CE |
| Prairie View Agricultural and Mechanical College of Texas(a) | | | |
| Prairie View | State | 2715 | CE Eng |
| Texas College(a) | | | |
| Tyler | CME, UNCF | 669 | CE |
| Texas Southern University(a) | | | |
| Houston | State | 3250 | CE |
| Wiley College(a) | | | |
| Marshall | Meth, UNCF | 514 | CE |
| | Junior Colleges | | |
| St. Phillips College(ja) | | | |
| San Antonio | Public | 1000 | CE |
| VIRGINIA | Senior Colleges | | |
| Hampton Institute(a) | | | |
| Hampton | Ind, UNCF | 1343 | CE BA |
| St. Paul's College(a) | | | |
| Lawrenceville | PE, UNCF | 417 | CE |
| Virginia State College(a) | | | |
| Petersburgh | State | 1500 | CE |
| Virginia Theological Seminary and College(b) | | | |
| Lynchburg | Bapt | 265 | CE |
| Virginia Union University(a) | | | |
| Richmond | Bapt, UNCF, Ind. | 856 | CE |
| WEST VIRGINIA | Senior Colleges | | |
| Bluefield State College(a) | | | |
| Bluefield | State | 550 | CE |
| West Virginia State College(a) | | | |
| Institute | State | 2057 | CE BA |

# KEY

Letters following school name:
- (a) Senior Institution having regional accreditation.
- (b) Senior Institution not having accreditation by one of six regional bodies.
- (ja) Junior Institution having regional accreditation.
- (jb) Junior Institution without regional accreditation.

Support

| | |
|---|---|
| AMA | American Missionary Association, Congregational |
| AME | African Methodist Episcopal Church |
| AMEZ | African Methodist Episcopal Zion Church |
| Bapt | Baptist Church |
| CME | Christian Methodist Episcopal Church |
| ELC | Evangelical Lutheran Synodical Conference of N.A. |
| Ind | Independent |
| Meth | Methodist Church |
| Munic | Municipal |
| PE | Protestant Episcopal Church |
| Pres | United Presbyterian Church in the U.S.A. |
| D. of C. | Disciples of Christ |
| Public | Municipal or state government |
| RC | Roman Catholic Church |
| SDA | Seventh-Day Adventists |
| State | State Government |
| Interd | Interdenominational |
| UNCF | United Negro College Fund |

Type

| | |
|---|---|
| CE | Coed |
| M | Male only |
| F | Women only |

Miscellaneous

| | |
|---|---|
| BA | Offers program in Business Administration |
| Eng | Offers program in engineering |

## Exhibit 5

Advertising Agencies That Have Responded to Mayor Robert Wagner's Committee on Job Advancement's Request for Cooperation in Placing Advertisements "Showing Representatives of Identifiable Minority Groups."*

N. W. Ayer and Son
Batten, Barton, Durstine and Osborn
Benton and Bowles
Harold Cabot and Company
Doyle Dane Bernbach
Durand Sapan Advertising
Foote, Cone, and Belding
Geyer, Morey, Ballard
Grey Advertising
Maxon Inc.
Mogul, Williams and Saylor
Sullivan, Stauffer, Colwell and Bayles
J. Walter Thompson Company
Young and Rubicam

---

*"Major Breakthrough in Integrated Ads," Advertising Age, 35:58, February 17, 1964.

Exhibit 6

# EXAMPLE OF CRITERIA NEGRO GROUPS USE
# WHEN SELECTING COMPANIES TO CONTACT

## *Criteria for Selecting Areas of Concentration*
## *For Job Development and Employment Activities*

Inasmuch as the Urban League has neither the staff or resources to cover the entire "waterfront" in developing new job openings, I am suggesting the following items for consideration in deciding "priorities." As you look at each item, ask yourself what you can do about it. It will be on the basis of your answer that you select your area of concentration.

1. Local or National operation.
2. Products—services or manufacturing.
3. Length of time in community.
4. Size of work force—men, women or both.
5. Is employment stable, expanding or decreasing?
6. Kinds of skills used.
7. Availability of skills (Negroes)
8. Training programs offered.
   a) In schools
   b) Under MDTA
   c) Availability of new training resources
9. Pre-employment training available.
10. Organized or not—what unions?
11. Government contract or "Plans for Progress."
12. Relationships of goods and services to Negro community in terms of use.
13. Availability of manpower to do survey—volunteers and staff.
14. Availability of manpower and resources for doing follow-up or action program.

National Urban League Skills Bank Form 170   11/1/63

Exhibit 7

POPULATION

Showing Total, White, Negro and Percent White and Negro
of Total 1960*

| City | 1960 Population | | | % White | % Negro |
| | Total | White | Negro | | |
|------|-------|-------|-------|---------|---------|
| Akron, Ohio | 290,351 | 252,457 | 37,636 | 86.9 | 13.0 |
| Anderson, Ind. | 49,061 | 44,674 | 4,337 | 91.1 | 8.8 |
| Atlanta, Ga. | 487,455 | 300,635 | 186,464 | 61.7 | 38.3 |
| Baltimore, Md. | 939,024 | 610,608 | 325,589 | 65.0 | 34.7 |
| Boston, Mass. | 697,197 | 628,704 | 63,165 | 90.2 | 9.1 |
| Buffalo, N.Y. | 532,759 | 459,371 | 70,904 | 86.2 | 13.3 |
| Canton, Ohio | 113,631 | 102,484 | 11,055 | 90.2 | 9.7 |
| Champaign, Ill. | 49,583 | 44,696 | 4,520 | 90.1 | 9.1 |
| Chicago, Ill. | 3,550,404 | 2,712,748 | 812,637 | 76.4 | 22.9 |
| Cincinnati, Ohio | 502,550 | 392,868 | 108,754 | 78.2 | 21.6 |
| Cleveland, Ohio | 876,050 | 622,942 | 250,818 | 71.1 | 28.6 |
| Columbus, Ohio | 471,316 | 393,011 | 77,140 | 83.4 | 16.4 |
| Dayton, Ohio | 262,332 | 204,785 | 57,288 | 78.1 | 21.8 |
| Denver, Colo. | 493,887 | 458,626 | 30,251 | 92.9 | 6.1 |
| Detroit, Mich. | 1,670,144 | 1,182,970 | 482,223 | 70.8 | 28.9 |
| Elizabeth, N.J. | 107,698 | 95,818 | 11,697 | 89.0 | 10.9 |
| Englewood, N.J. | 26,057 | 18,942 | 7,008 | 72.7 | 26.9 |
| Flint, Mich. | 196,940 | 162,128 | 34,521 | 82.3 | 17.5 |
| Ft. Wayne, Ind. | 161,776 | 149,787 | 11,645 | 92.6 | 7.2 |
| Gary, Ind. | 178,320 | 108,980 | 69,123 | 61.1 | 38.8 |
| Grand Rapids, Mich. | 177,313 | 162,535 | 14,260 | 91.7 | 8.0 |
| Jacksonville, Fla. | 201,030 | 118,286 | 82,525 | 58.8 | 41.1 |
| Kansas City, Mo. | 475,539 | 391,348 | 83,146 | 82.3 | 17.5 |
| Little Rock, Ark. | 107,813 | 82,461 | 25,286 | 76.5 | 23.5 |
| Los Angeles, Calif. | 2,479,015 | 2,011,808 | 334,916 | 81.2 | 13.5 |
| Louisville, Ky. | 390,639 | 320,190 | 70,075 | 82.0 | 17.9 |
| Marion, Ind. | 37,854 | 34,903 | 2,901 | 92.2 | 7.7 |
| Massillon, Ohio | 31,236 | 28,501 | 2,718 | 91.2 | 8.7 |
| Memphis, Tenn. | 497,524 | 312,799 | 184,320 | 62.9 | 37.0 |
| Miami, Fla. | 291,688 | 225,888 | 65,213 | 77.4 | 22.4 |
| Milwaukee, Wisc. | 741,324 | 675,572 | 62,458 | 91.1 | 8.4 |
| Minneapolis, Minn. | 482,872 | 467,278 | 11,785 | 96.8 | 2.4 |
| Morristown, N.J. | 17,712 | 15,167 | 2,488 | 85.6 | 14.0 |
| Muskegon, Mich. | 46,485 | 42,670 | 3,685 | 91.8 | 7.9 |
| Newark, N.J. | 405,220 | 265,889 | 138,035 | 65.6 | 34.1 |

*U.S. Department of Commerce, Bureau of the Census

Exhibit 7 (continued)

| City | 1960 Population | | | % White | % Negro |
|------|------|------|------|------|------|
| | Total | White | Negro | | |
| New Brunswick, N.J. | 40,139 | 33,810 | 6,187 | 84.2 | 15.4 |
| New Haven, Conn. | 152,048 | 129,325 | 22,079 | 85.0 | 14.5 |
| New Orleans, La. | 627,525 | 392,594 | 233,514 | 62.6 | 37.2 |
| New York, N.Y. | 7,781,984 | 6,640,662 | 1,087,931 | 85.3 | 14.0 |
| Oklahoma City, Okla. | 324,253 | 281,971 | 37,529 | 87.0 | 11.6 |
| Omaha, Nebraska | 301,598 | 275,330 | 25,155 | 91.3 | 8.3 |
| Philadelphia, Pa. | 2,002,512 | 1,467,479 | 529,240 | 73.3 | 26.4 |
| Phoenix, Ariz. | 439,170 | 413,519 | 20,919 | 94.2 | 5.8 |
| Pittsburgh, Pa. | 604,332 | 502,593 | 100,692 | 83.2 | 16.7 |
| Pontiac, Mich. | 82,233 | 68,256 | 13,744 | 83.0 | 16.7 |
| Portland, Ore. | 372,676 | 351,757 | 15,637 | 94.4 | 4.2 |
| Providence, R.I. | 207,498 | 195,525 | 11,153 | 94.2 | 5.4 |
| Richmond, Va. | 219,958 | 127,627 | 91,972 | 58.0 | 41.8 |
| St. Louis, Mo. | 750,026 | 534,004 | 214,377 | 71.2 | 29.6 |
| St. Paul, Minn. | 313,411 | 304,094 | 8,240 | 97.0 | 2.6 |
| San Diego, Calif. | 573,224 | 528,512 | 34,435 | 92.2 | 6.0 |
| San Francisco, Calif. | 740,316 | 604,403 | 74,383 | 81.6 | 10.0 |
| Oakland, Calif. | 367,548 | 270,523 | 83,618 | 73.6 | 22.8 |
| Seattle, Wash. | 557,087 | 510,559 | 26,901 | 91.6 | 4.8 |
| South Bend, Ind. | 132,445 | 119,276 | 12,955 | 90.1 | 9.8 |
| Springfield, Ill. | 83,271 | 77,572 | 5,632 | 93.2 | 6.8 |
| Springfield, Mass. | 174,463 | 161,102 | 13,080 | 92.3 | 7.5 |
| Springfield, Ohio | 82,723 | 70,822 | 11,838 | 85.6 | 14.3 |
| Tampa, Fla. | 274,970 | 228,514 | 46,244 | 83.1 | 16.8 |
| Tulsa, Okla. | 261,685 | 235,620 | 22,489 | 90.0 | 8.6 |
| Warren, Ohio | 59,648 | 52,751 | 6,855 | 88.4 | 11.5 |
| Washington, D. C. | 763,956 | 345,263 | 411,737 | 45.2 | 53.9 |
| White Plains, N.Y. | 50,485 | 44,486 | 5,880 | 88.1 | 11.6 |
| Wichita, Kans. | 254,698 | 233,539 | 19,861 | 91.7 | 7.8 |
| Winston-Salem, N.C. | 11,135 | 69,895 | 41,185 | 62.9 | 37.1 |

| | |
|------|------|
| Total Population, United States | 179,323,175 |
| Negro Population, United States | 18,871,831 |
| Percent Negro to Total | 10.5 |

Prepared by Research Department, National Urban League
February, 1963

# BIBLIOGRAPHY

PAMPHLETS

*General Background*

The American Dream...Equal Opportunity, Report on the Community Leaders' Conference Sponsored by President's Committee on Equal Employment Opportunity, Washington, D. C.,
May 19, 1962, 56 pages.

Clark, Kenneth B., The Negro Protest, Boston, Beacon Press,
1963, 56 pages.

Enion, Richard A., and Homan, Halward L., "What Are Some
Industrial Relations Approaches to Integration?," Personnel
Administration, 26:55-57, November-December, 1963.
Integration is inevitable in industry; management, there-
fore, would be well advised to become an active participant in
shaping policies of integration.

"Improving Industrial Race Relations," Personnel Administration,
26:25-31, March-April, 1963.
Advice to personnel managers regarding human relations
problems when integrating. A good analysis of the Negro's
view of a company.

"The Negro Drive for More Jobs; What It Means To Business,"
Business Week, August 17, 1963, p. 52.
The most comprehensive survey of business integration at
the end of the summer of 1963. Good discussion of pressures
(Government and Negro) placed on business. Several interest-
ing case studies.

The New Dimension of the Negro Market, New York, A. Bernard
Howard and Company, Inc., Presentation, 1962.
   An appraisal of Negro buying power in 15 major metro-
politan market areas by an organization that represents many
Negro program radio stations.

Norgen, Paul H., "Racial Discrimination in Employment,"
Selected References, Industrial Relations Section, Princeton
University, No. 107, September, 1962.
   A bibliography of books and articles related to racial
discrimination.

Weaver, Robert C., The Negro as an American, New York, Center
for the Study of Democratic Institutions of the Fund for the
Republic, Inc., 1963, 9 pages.
   Explains Negro problems in terms of historical and
present-day situations. Points to Negro demands as a matter
of "right," not "merit." Dispels many erroneous beliefs about
Negroes. Discusses discrimination as providing Negroes with
an excuse for failure.

"What Helps or Harms Promotability," Harvard Business Review,
42:6-8, January, 1964.
   Reports what businessmen think are the personal background qualities which help and hinder management integration,
including an appraisal of effects of Negroes as managers, and
the role of business and businessmen in achieving equality of
management opportunity.

## Economic Factors

Becker, Gary S., The Economics of Discrimination, Chicago,
University of Chicago Press, 1957, 137 pages.
   A quantitative analysis of the cost of discrimination. Takes
into consideration the effect of discrimination on the income of
employers, employees, consumers, and governments.

"A Century of Change: Negroes in the U.S. Economy, 1860-1960,"
Monthly Labor Review, December, 1962, v. 85, No. 12, pp. 1359-
1365.
   Traces changes in health, education, occupation level, and
income of Negroes.

The Economic Situation of Negroes in the U.S., U.S Department of
Labor, Bulletin S-3, U.S. Government Printing Office, Revised,
1962, President's Committee on Equal Employment Opportunity,
32 pages.
   Statistical treatment of Negro economic situation. Discussion of Negro's legal rights and the legal obligation of a company.

The Negro Wage-Earner and Apprenticeship Training Programs, Labor Department, 1960, 60 pages.

Detailed study of the need for many additional skilled craftsmen, of the barriers presently preventing the Negro from participating in apprenticeship programs, and of the necessity for permitting Negroes to join these programs.

## Government Documents

Executive Orders 10925 and 11114, U.S. Government Printing Office 694-467, 1963, President's Committee on Equal Employment Opportunity.

Orders setting up the President's Committee on Equal Employment Opportunity, outlining its functions, and laying down compliance procedures for defense contractors.

Rules and Regulations of the President's Committee on Equal Employment Opportunity, Published by the President's Committee on Equal Employment Opportunity, Washington, D. C., U.S. Government Printing Office, 1963, 0-705-326, 22 pages.

Southern Regional Council, Plans for Progress: Atlanta Survey, Atlanta, January 1963, 15 pages.

A brief history of the Plans for Progress followed by a comprehensive survey of the reactions to and actions taken in view of the Plans for Progress by twenty-four Southern branches of Plans for Progress signers. Clearly demonstrates the need for top management commitment and the necessity of demonstrating this commitment to the rest of the corporation.

## Implementation Suggestions

Bird, Caroline, "More Room at the Top," Management Review, 52:4-16, March 1963.

An excellent account of the experiences of several companies that have employed Negroes in professional and management jobs. Lays down general guidelines, empirically developed, for the transition from segregated to integrated operations.

Borgeson, Roger D , Norgren, Paul H., Patten, Maud B., Webster, Albert N., Employing the Negro in American Industry, New York, Industrial Relations Counselors, Inc., 1959.

A useful text containing a detailed description of how to implement an integration program.

Calvert, Robert Jr., How To Recruit Minority Group College Graduates, Swarthmore, Pa., The Personnel Journal, Inc., 1963, 42 pages.

A helpful guide to recruiting educated and skilled minority group members.

"Improving Industrial Race Relations—Equal Job Opportunity, Slogan or Reality?," Personnel Administration, 26:25-32, March-April, 1963.

Explains why equal job opportunity is not a reality and calls for the support of personnel workers in government and private industry to reverse the situation.

Kheel, Theodore W., "How Race Relations Affect Your Business," Labor Report Bulletin, No. 7, August 15, 1963.

One of the most thorough published discussions of racial integration in business. Particularly useful to government contractors. General background of race relations problems in business. Detailed analysis of the requirements of government contractors under the President's Committee on Equal Employment. Includes specific experiences which occurred under the committee when the author served as advisor to its chairman, then Vice President Johnson.

Morrow, J. J., "American Negroes—A Wasted Resource," Harvard Business Review, 35:65-74, January-February, 1957.

A study of the opportunities, problems, advantages and disadvantages of business hiring more Negroes. An excellent article containing many examples and worthwhile suggestions for the development of corporate plans.

Perry, John, "Business—Next Target for Integration," Harvard Business Review, March-April, 1963.

Best, most comprehensive article on business integration we have seen. Suggests logical, practical methods of integration. Excellent discussion of the concept of "place." Excellent as means of acquainting managers with the problems.

Robinson, Jackie, "The Racial Crisis," Sales Management, 91:33-37, August 16, 1963.

Advice to American Business from an individual who is able to understand the problems of the Negro and the businessman.

"Self-Analysis Questionnaire," U.S. Bureau of the Budget, No. 44-R1174.

An excellent outline of a Self-Analysis Questionnaire which should reveal problem areas within a company. Excellent document from which to develop an internal reporting device.

## Services Providing Useful Information

Turk, Leonard, Management and Minority Manpower, 210 E. 47th Street, New York, New York 10017.

A four page, high quality, biweekly service that reviews general trends since last issue and contains a bibliography of pertinent articles and programs. Cost: $25 per year.

American Negro Reference Guide, New York, New York, World
   Mutual Exchange, Inc., 79 Wall Street New York 5, New York.
   A monthly reference magazine for keeping current with
   the Negro market. Contains:
   1. Annotated listing of Negro newspapers, magazines
      and publications.
   2. Listing of Negro program radio stations.
   3. Annotated listing of Negro colleges.
   4. Annotated reference to current articles about the
      Negro market.
   Cost: $10 per year.

## PERIODICALS AND NEWSPAPERS

### *General Background*

"America's 100 Most Influential Negroes," Ebony, 18:228-232,
   September, 1963.

"Anti-Bias Drive," Business Week, March 5, 1960, p. 54.
   A discussion with George Meany on the problems and
   progress of integration in labor unions.

"Bias in Reverse?," Wall Street Journal, 162:1, August 12, 1962.
   White workers claim employers now show favoritism to
   Negroes.

"Civil Rights: The Moral Crisis," Time, 81:13-18, June 21, 1963.
   It is time to act in all of our daily lives.

"CORE Seeks More Integrated Ads--NAACP Tells 4 A's of 5 Point
   Program," Advertising Age, 34:1, September 9, 1963.
   Describes the pressures that have been placed on adver-
   tising agencies and companies with large advertising budgets.
   Details are included of success to date.

Haseldon, Kyle, and Whitney M. Young, Jr., "Should There Be
   Compensation for Negroes," New York Times Magazine, p. 43,
   October 6, 1963. An excellent discussion of both sides of this
   issue.

"How Whites Feel About Negroes," Newsweek, 62:44-50, October
   21, 1963.
   A survey of 1260 white Americans throughout the United
   States to objectively determine their current sentiments about
   Negroes.

"Is Race a Problem All Over the U.S.?," U.S. News and World
   Report, 55:68-72, October 21, 1963.
   Discussion of racial tensions outside the South. Describes
   Northern attitude of equality-at-a-distance.

"Jobs for Negroes: How Much Progress in Sight," Newsweek,
   62:68-70, July 15, 1963.
      A summary of the present situation with Negro employ-
   ment and predictions about future.

"Just How Well Off Is the American Negro?," U.S. News and
   World Report, 55:44-45, July 22, 1963.
      Description of Negro economic gains since the beginning
   of World War II and of the Negro's present economic situation.

"Negro Force in the Market Place," Business Week, May 25, 1962,
   p. 75.
      Discussion of various approaches taken by companies to
   reach the Negro market. Attacks the question of whether or
   not it is a separate market and whether or not a different
   approach is needed.

"The Negro in America," Newsweek, 62:15-36, July 29, 1963.
      The findings of a poll of over 1250 interviews with
   Negroes: Their desires, their plans, their leaders, what they
   think of whites, their willingness to take action, and what they
   expect in the future. An article that can help in understanding
   the Negro.

"Negro Leaders Tell Their Plans for 1964," U.S. News and World
   Report, 56:56-62, February 24, 1964.
      Interviews with leaders of National Urban League,
   Southern Christian Leadership Conference, NAACP, CORE,
   and SNCC.
      All place the opening up of employment opportunities high
   on their lists of priorities.

"Races-Freedom-Now," Time, 81:23-27, May 17, 1963.
      General background article on the civil rights situation
   in the United States.

"The Risks of Impatience," The Wall Street Journal, October 19,
   1963, p. 12.
      Discussion of demanding integration too rapidly, particu-
   larly by Negro groups with respect to industry.

Silberman, Charles, "The City and the Negro," Fortune, March,
   1962, p. 88ff.
      An excellent and thorough analysis of the plight of the
   Negro city dweller and his effect on the future of cities. Includes a plea for "positive discrimination."

U.S News and World Report, 54:33-34, June 24, 1963.
      Trilogy on rising racial tensions. The need for jobs of all
   kinds for all, and the part this plays in racial tensions. Instances of peaceful, voluntary desegregation in the South.

"What the American Negro Wants," <u>U.S. News and World Report</u>,
54:46-52, April 29, 1963
    An interview with Roy Wilkins. Discussion of what the
Negro has, what he wants, his present mood, and how he is
trying to advance the cause.

"When a Negro Faces North," <u>Look</u>, 27:30-62, December 17, 1963.
    A series of articles that deal with housing, community
relations, employment, and the responsibility of business.

White, Theodore H., "Power Structure, Integration, Militancy,
Freedom Now!," <u>Life</u>, November 29, 1963, pp. 78-93.
    A general background article surveying actions and appeals
of civil rights groups.

## *Industry Background*

"Bringing Better Jobs to Negroes," <u>Business Week</u>, November 3,
1962, p. 134.
    Description of the activities of the Harvey Executive Place-
ment Company, Philadelphia, Pa. Places both Negroes and
whites in executive positions in industry. Is operated by a
Negro.

Chase, Edward T., "Quotas for Negroes," <u>The Commonweal</u>,
79:451-454, January 17, 1964.
    "If quotas and preferential hiring are disallowed, it is
hard to see how much will be accomplished for Negro employment."

"Crashing Gates to Better Jobs," <u>Business Week</u>, June 22, 1963,
p. 24.
    Story of the hiring of Mr. Harvey Russell, a Negro, by
Pepsi-Cola to serve as a Vice President in charge of "Special
Markets."

"Forced Hiring of Negroes—How It Would Work," <u>U.S. News and
World Report</u>, 55:83-84, July 29, 1963.
    How civil rights laws with respect to employment might
be enforced by the National Government.

"Hiring, Firing, Promoting, Unions Policing Ahead," <u>U. S. News
and World Report</u>, 55:107-109, November 11, 1963.
    How the Federal Government could enforce the provisions
of new measures before Congress to prevent job discrimina-
tions.

"How Negro Pressures Get Jobs," <u>U.S. News and World Report</u>,
55:28-32, August 12, 1963.
    How a selective patronage program works and its record
of success.

"Jobs for Negroes—Is There a Real Shortage?," U.S. News and World Report, 55:28-30, August 12, 1963.
"Negroes with skills are hard to find all across the U.S.," report many firms that are now trying to hire Negroes.

Kuebler, Jeanne, "Negro Jobs and Education," Editorial Research Reports, pp. 47-64, January 23, 1963.
Improvements in job openings for Negroes. Obstacles to employment of Negroes; progress towards educational equality; action to foster equal opportunity.

"Negroes Are Moving Up the Job Ladder," Reader's Digest, 83:53-57, December, 1963.
General article describing several incidents where there have been expanded opportunities made available to Negroes.

"Negroes Use Stock Ownership as Civil Rights Tool," Wall Street Journal, 1:5, January 2, 1964.
Discussion of a plan formulated by Negroes to obtain stock in restaurant chains and other retail businesses in order to force integration through voting power.

"Science and the Race Problem," Science, 142:558-561, November 1, 1963.
A report of the American Association for the Advancement of Science—Committee on Science in the Promotion of Human Welfare.
Conclusion: There is no valid scientific evidence to support claims that the Negro race is biologically inferior.

Silberman, Charles, "The Businessman and the Negro," Fortune, 68:96-99, September, 1963.
An excellent article that provides a considerable amount of background material on integration and its effect on business.

Smith, Dan, "Help Wanted: Negroes," Electronics, 37:95-96, March 23, 1964.
The problems of hiring and recruiting qualified Negroes for highly technical jobs.

## Implementation Suggestions

Brooks, T. R., "Managing Your Manpower-Negro Employment Problems," Duns Review, 82:59-60, August, 1963.
A discussion of several integration problems and how the Urban League has helped business to solve them.

"Carrying Out a Plan for Job Integration," Business Week, April
13, 1963, pp. 90-96.
    Lockheed Georgia's experience with integration. Discus-
sion of government pressures on defense contractors. Tells
how one company integrated with only minor hardships through
firm and deliberate action.

Cox, Ted, "Counselor's Views on Changing Management Policies,"
Public Relations Journal, 19:8-9, November, 1963.
    Deals with the responsibility of the public relations group
to help business meet the problems of discrimination.

"Guidelines for Initiating Fair Employment Practices," Personnel,
May-June 1963, pp. 53-59.
    Summary of considerations for personnel departments
supervising integration.

"A New Form for Employers to Struggle With," U.S. News and
World Report, 52:104ff, February 12, 1962.
    Description of compliance form for defense contractors,
its use and possible enforcement procedures.

Shostak, Arthur B., "Improving Industrial Race Relations—Human
Problems in Improving Industrial Race Relations," Personnel
Administration, 26:25-32, March-April, 1963.
    This article includes discussion and some suggested solu-
tions for potential problems that employers may have when
placed under government pressure to integrate. A good discussion of the damage done by reverse discrimination is also
included.